The Proper Care of
COCKATOOS

Photo by Michael DeFreitas.

Major Mitchell's Cockatoo, the red Cockatoos and Sulphur-crested Cockatoos (those with the sulphur-colored crest), freely interbreed in zoos in Australia and many of these and many of the hybrids are on display. Photo courtesy of Vogelpark Walsorode, Germany.

The Proper Care of
COCKATOOS

Helmut Pinter

Distributed in the UNITED STATES to the Pet Trade by T.F.H. Publications, Inc., One T.F.H. Plaza, Neptune City, NJ 07753; distributed in the UNITED STATES to the Bookstore and Library Trade by National Book Network, Inc. 4720 Boston Way, Lanham MD 20706; in CANADA to the Pet Trade by H & L Pet Supplies Inc., 27 Kingston Crescent, Kitchener, Ontario N2B 2T6; Rolf C. Hagen Ltd., 3225 Sartelon Street, Montreal 382 Quebec; in CANADA to the Book Trade by Macmillan of Canada (A Division of Canada Publishing Corporation), 164 Commander Boulevard, Agincourt, Ontario M1S 3C7; in ENGLAND by T.F.H. Publications, PO Box 15, Waterlooville PO7 6BQ; in AUSTRALIA AND THE SOUTH PACIFIC by T.F.H. (Australia), Pty. Ltd., Box 149, Brookvale 2100 N.S.W., Australia; in NEW ZEALAND by Brooklands Aquarium Ltd., 5 McGiven Drive, New Plymouth, RD1 New Zealand; in the PHILIPPINES by Bio-Research, 5 Lippay Street, San Lorenzo Village, Makati, Rizal; in SOUTH AFRICA by Multipet Pty. Ltd., P.O. Box 35347, Northway, 4065, South Africa. Published by T.F.H. Publications, Inc. Manufactured in the United States of America by T.F.H. Publications, Inc.

CONTENTS

Cockatoos were first introduced to modern civilization 750 years ago but native peoples throughout the region of Cockatoos have made companions of them...probably for the past 10,000 years. Cockatoos might very well have been the first bird s to become pets. Photo by Robert Pearcy.

Introduction

The first historically verified Cockatoo to arrive alive in Europe was sent as a gift by a Saracen Sultan about the year 1250 to the Emperor of the Holy Roman Empire of German States, Frederick II von Hohenstaufen. Frederick, a grandson of Frederick Barbarossa, or

Redbeard, was an excellent bird fancier. His palace contained several animal enclosures and pheasant preserves. We don't know exactly what kind of Cockatoo was sent as this gift. Based upon Saracen trade connections of that day, it seems probable that it was a small yellow-headed Cockatoo, likely a Lesser Sulphur-crested Cockatoo, *Cacatua sulphurea*.

Somewhat later, mention of crested white parrots is found in the travel reports of the Venetian Marco Polo (1254–1324), who came across them as cage birds in southern India. This fact is interesting because there are no Cockatoos native to India. These birds were apparently brought from Indonesia as household animals. Mention of Cockatoos in their natural habitat was made by another Venetian, Nicolo de Conto, who, in a 1441 report about the Moluccan Islands, claims witness to a white Cockatoo of the size of a hen, as well as other parrots.

The first truly practical descriptions of the Cockatoo came from the pen of the Zurich dentist and naturalist Conrad Gesner (1516–1605). Yet, the illustrations that were published with these descriptions suggest that the Cockatoo was known only through hearsay. Other illustrations, however,

Facing page: Goffin's Cockatoo, Cacatua goffini, was an early favorite amongst bird-lovers. The original descriptions of Cockatoos is credited to Conrad Gesner (1516-1605).

indicate that Cockatoos did reach Europe alive, although probably only one at a time. An example is a life-sized Sulphur-crested Cockatoo depicted in *Madonna della Vittoria*, painted by Andrea Mantegna in 1496 in Mantua. Large numbers of Cockatoos began to arrive in Europe only after the Dutch and the English established regular shipping routes to Indonesia and Australia from about 1700 on. Today the Cockatoo enjoys world-wide recognition and is among the most highly prized of companion animals.

Lovers of birds usually don't stop with a single species. Often Cockatoos are found in the same home as other parrots, like Amazons, Budgerigars and Cockatiels. Photo by Michael DeFreitas.

The most popular parrot is the Cockatiel. This bird is closely related to the Cockatoo because they are both parrots and both have the erectile crest. They are, however, much smaller and have been bred in many color varieties. Photo of a juvenile Cockatiel by Robert Pearcy.

Cockatoo Species

Cockatoos belong to the subfamily Cacatuinae in the order of parrots, Psittaciformes. They are distinguished from other parrots by their erectable crest, easily recognized even by beginners. (The smaller Cockatiel, which also has a similar feather crest, is related to the

1.

2.

3.

1. *The Lesser Sulphur-crested Cockatoo*, Cacatua sulphurea citrinocristata.
2. *The Black Cockatoo* Calyptorhynchus funereus baudinii.
3. *The Galah*, Eolophus roseicapillus.
4. *The Palm Cockatoo* Probosciger aterimmus.
5. *Goffin's Cockatoo*, Cacatua goffini.
6. *The Black Cockatoo* Calyptorhynchus funereus funereus.
Photos courtesy of Vogelpark Walsrode, Germany.

Cockatoos and is often kept as a cage bird.) Cockatoos are relatively large parrots with 12- to 28-inch body lengths; thus, some Cockatoos rank among the largest of parrots. Certain species have long been kept as indoor pets not only in Europe and America but also in their native lands. As far as speech goes, Cockatoos can only rarely measure up to Amazons or African Greys, although there are individual Cockatoos who are very good talkers. Besides having an impressive appearance, Cockatoos are valued by fanciers as gentle and good-natured creatures that can be tamed easily. Properly handled, many Cockatoos learn little tricks. Such trained Cockatoos used to be seen often at fairs and in stage acts. Cockatoos can

4.

5.

6.

1.

2.

3.

1. *Major Mitchell's Cockatoo,* Cacatua leadbeateri.
2. *The Salmon-crested Cockatoo,* Cacatua moluccensis.
3. *The Lesser Sulphur-crested Cockatoo* Cacatua sulphurea parvula.
4. *The White Cockatoo,* Cacatua alba.
5. *The Red-vented Cockatoo,* Cacatua haematuropygia.
6. *The Cockatiel is not a true Cockatoo, but it has many features in common with Cockatoos such as the erectile crest and the cheek marking. It is also a parrot-family bird.*
Photos by Vogelpark Walsrode, Germany.

live for an amazingly long time. Maximal age depends roughly upon size. Individual birds cf the largest species have been known to live as long as 90 years, while members of the smaller species tend to have considerably shorter life spans. Once acclimated to their home, most Cockatoos are quite modest in needs and easy to keep. Since in nature they feed to a large extent on seeds and fruit, they do not cause any great difficulties in feeding in captivity.

Cockatoos breed well in captivity, in comparison to other parrots. Hobbyists succeed relatively often in breeding many Cockatoo species. Thanks to these birds born in captivity, even a few Australian species are available now and then, despite the present ban on

4.

5.

6.

the exportation of native Australian Cockatoos.

The Cockatoo subfamily comprises a total of 17 species in 5 genera. Those of greatest interest to the bird lover are mainly the so-called White Cockatoos of the genus *Cacatua*. The 11 species of this genus have a predominantly white or very light plumage, and a few of them have a

The Little Corella Cacatua sanguinea sanguinea. *Photo by Vogelpark Walsrode, Germany.*

pure white plumage. Of the species belonging to the remaining genera, only the Rose-breasted Cockatoo of the (sub)genus *Eolophus* is kept any longer as a household bird. Some Cockatoos, such as the Palm Cockatoo (*Probosciger atterrimus*), Black Cockatoos *(Calyptorhynchus* spp.), and the peculiar Helmeted, or Gang-Gang, Cockatoo *(Callocephalon fimbriatum)*, are today either protected by the Washington Agreement (CITES) or else fall under export prohibitions by Australian regulations. Needless to say, these species can no longer be marketed. You can see these species, however, in many zoos, where some of them have been successfully bred.

The areas in which Cockatoos live natively can be precisely delineated on a map. Besides their natural range of distribution, in two localiities they were introduced by man: Lesser Sulphur-crested Cockatoos are found today in the vicinity of Singapore, and Greater Sulphur-cresteds are naturalized in New Zealand. Wild Cockatoos are seen either in small groups or in large swarms. Climate and landscape of the ranges are quite varied, from the humid rain forests of Indonesia and New Guinea for example, to very arid regions in Australia.

The Gang-gang Cockatoo, Callocephalon fimbriatum. Photo by Vogelpark Walsrode, Germany.

All Cockatoos breed in hollows of tree trunks or similar places. They clear out and enlarge decayed or damaged trunks to the desired size with their powerful bills. Brooding pairs often keep aloof from others of their group.

All Cockatoos can fly well and with endurance. Large flocks of those birds inhabiting arid regions (such as the Rose-breast) are capable of undertaking long migrations.

The diet of wild Cockatoos in nature is extremely varied. Besides seeds of every kind, they eat many green plants and many also eat insects. Species from extremely arid regions partially satisfy their need for water by eating green plant parts. Because of the often monotonous diet in arid regions, one finds real dietary specialists among the Australian species. Cockatoos from rain forests and other areas with profuse vegetation and varied food sources are less specialized. Among the species with less-specialized diets are the birds that are easiest to keep as household pets.

Let us now review the Cockatoos which are kept as household cage and aviary birds, including some of the rarer species.

Little Corellas are powerful fliers. They can cover long distances and usually scream as they fly. They are very 'scary' and take flight as soon as they perceive any danger. This photos was taken in their natural habitat in Australia. Photo courtesy of Vogelpark Walrode, Germany.

MAJOR MITCHELL'S COCKATOO
(Cacatua leadbeateri)

Major Mitchell's Cockatoo is from the dry interior regions of Australia. There are two subspecies which differ only slightly from one another *(C. l. mollis* lacks a yellow band in the feather crest). Length is about 15 inches. Throat, breast and abdomen are salmon pink. Wings are white and light reddish above, salmon pink below. Crest is red, yellow and white. The sexes can be told apart by the iris color: very dark, almost black in the male, and brownish red in the female.

Almost all Cockatoos kept in captivity belong to *C. l. leadbeateri. Since* export of these birds is prohibited, and export licenses from the Australian Natural

On Guadalcanal and many of the other islands in the region, the local people collect the Ducorps's Cockatoo, Cacatua ducorpsii, when they are babies, and raise them as house pets, usually allowing them free flight. They once had a wonderful business doing this but international regulations soon put a stop to it. Photo courtesy of Vogelpark Walsrode, Germany.

Lesser Sulphur-crested Cockatoo, *Cacatua sulphurea.*

Opposite: Cockatoo Topography

1-Crest, 2-Crown, 3-Eye ring (sometimes present), 4-Forehead, 5-Lores, 6-Cheek, 7-Chin, 8-Neck, 9-Upper breast, 10-Lower breast, 11-Belly, 12-Foot, 13-Toe, 14-Vent, 15-Under tail coverts, 16-Eyebrow (sometimes present), 17-Occiput, 18-Nape, 19-Bend of the wing, 20-Shoulder feathers, 21-Back, 22-Lesser wing coverts, 23-Median wing coverts, 24-Greater wing coverts, 25-Lower back, 26-Flight coverts, 27-Rump, 28 Flightfeathers, 29-Upper tail coverts, 30-Tail feathers.

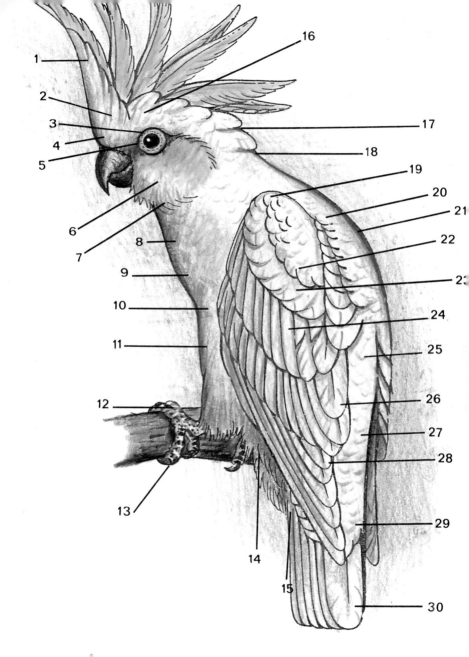

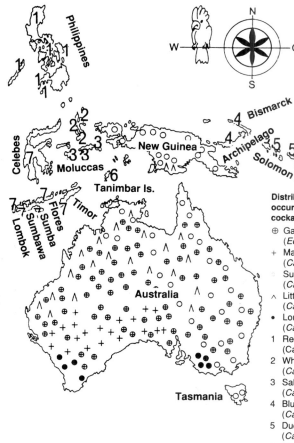

Distribution map showing the occurrence of the "light" cockatoo species.

⊕ Galah
   (*Eolophus roseicapillus*)
+ Major Mitchell's Cockatoo
   (*Cacatua leadbeateri*)
○ Sulphur-crested Cockatoo
   (*Cacatua galerita*)
∧ Little Corella
   (*Cacatua sanguinea*)
● Long-billed Corella
   (*Cacatua tenuirostris*)
1 Red-vented Cockatoo
   (*Cacatua haematuropygia*)
2 White Cockatoo
   (*Cacatua alba*)
3 Salmon-crested Cockatoo
   (*Cacatua moluccensis*)
4 Blue-eyed Cockatoo
   (*Cacatua ophtalmica*)
5 Ducorps's Cockatoo
   (*Cacatua ducorpsii*)
6 Goffin's Cockatoo
   (*Cacatua goffini*)
7 Lesser Sulphur-crested Cockatoo
   (*Cacatua sulphurea*)

A large flock of Cockatoos leaving a tree in Australia. There are many Cockatoos still to be found in Australia, thanks to the intelligent preservation of native species. Many Australian farmers are said to shoot the birds because they are so destructive to fruit trees. Photo by Ken Stepnell.

Conservation Authorities are granted only for accredited zoos, the birds are very rare in captivity. From time to time, however, birds bred in captivity are offered for sale, but the price is high. It would be irresponsible to keep as household pets the few birds of this species that remain, and all available birds should be reserved for breeding attempts.

A breeding pair of Major Mitchell's Cockatoos. The female has a red iris and more yellow in her crest. Photo courtesy of Vogelpark Walsrode, Germany. If you ever get to Germany you should visit the Walsrode Vogelpark (bird park). It is really magnificent.

Cacatua Leadbeateri, *Major Mitchell's Cockatoo. Photo by John Daniel.*

The habitat in which Major Mitchell's Cockatoos dwell has been so reduced by human activities that the wonderful Australian government has taken drastic steps to save this Cockatoo from extinction. Extinction is forever! Photo by Keith Hindwood.

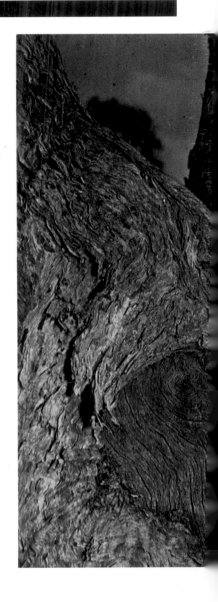

LESSER SULPHUR-CRESTED COCKATOO
(Cacatua sulphurea)

The Lesser Sulphur-crested Cockatoo and its subspecies live on the Celebes, Buton, and Sunda Islands, as well as islands in the Flores and Java Seas, Indonesia. The subspecies are difficult to tell apart, especially when their origins are unknown. At any rate, the Sunda Island subspecies *C. s. citrinocristata* (the *Citron*-crested or Lemon-crested Cockatoo) can be differentiated from the other subspecies by its orange-colored crest.

The length of a Lesser

Above: *A Lesser Sulphur-crested Cockatoo, Cacatua sulphurea. Photo by Carol Thiem.*

Facing page: *Major Mitchell's Cockatoo, Cacatua leadbeateri. This bird is a female as evidenced by the yellow band in her crest. Photo by Robert Pearcy.*

The Cockatoo shown above and the Cockatoo shown on the facing page are both subspecies of Cacatua sulphurea. The difference in their crest colors indicates they are subspecies. The lighter colored crest is C. s. parvula while the Cockatoo shown above is C. s. citrinocristata. Photo on the facing page by T. Tilford; the photo above is by Michael DeFreitas.

Sulphur-crested Cockatoo can be as much as 13 or 14 inches, but there are many smaller ones as well. The upper part of the plumage is white, the underside of the wings and the tail feathers are yellow. Crest and ear patches are likewise yellow. In the Citron-crested Cockatoo, the crest feathers are orange. The eye ring is white. The gray-black bill is generally more massive in the male than in the female. Sexually mature birds can be told apart by the different iris coloration: almost black in males and reddish brown in females.

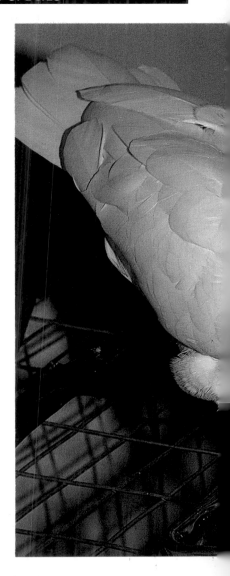

Lesser Sulphur-crested Cockatoo, Cacatua sulphurea, *having a meal of fresh vegetables. Photo by Carol Thiem.*

The Lesser Sulphur-crested Cockatoo is probably the most frequently kept of the Cockatoos today. The species has been bred successfully, and Sulphur-cresteds have successfully cared for their broods even in large wire cages. In essence, the majority of them are charming and easily approachable.

Right: A young Lesser Sulphur-crested Cockatoo, Cacatua sulphurea parvula, eating an apple. Photo by Robert Pearcy.

Facing page: Mutual preening by a pair(?) of Lesser Sulphur-crested Cockatoos, Cacatua sulphurea parvula. Photo by Ralph Kaehler.

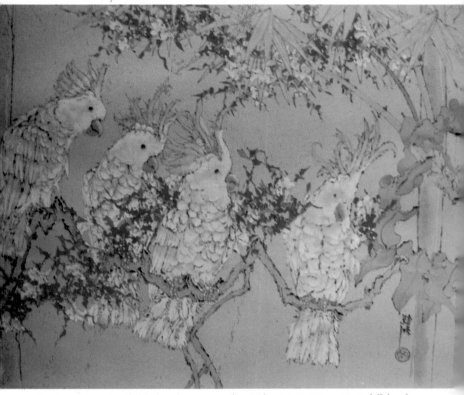

During an art exhibit in Singapore (1990) a tapestry was exhibited which featured four sulphur-crested Cockatoos. Photo by Dr. Herbert R. Axelrod.

SULPHUR-CRESTED COCKATOO

(Cacatua galerita)

It is difficult to tell the Australian subspecies apart. Those from New Guinea and the Aru Islands can be distinguished by their somewhat smaller size and the different coloration of the naked eye ring. The Australian subspecies attain a length of about 20 inches and have white eye rings; the eye rings of the other two subspecies are blue, and their length is only 18 inches at the most. Also, birds of Australian origin often exhibit yellow ear markings. The subspecies *C. g. triton* from New Guinea is called the Triton Cockatoo. Plumage color is white; wings and tail feathers are yellowish underneath. Almost always it's the Triton Cockatoo

A White Cockatoo, Cacatua alba with its crest extended, 'talking' to a Sulphur-crested Cockatoo.

which is offered for sale.

Sulphur-cresteds usually tame rapidly but are sometimes strongly attached to a single person. Also, their loud voice can easily disrupt the household. Their reproduction in aviaries is not difficult, and from time to time young birds of the Australian subspecies are offered for sale.

Above: The yellow crested bird is a Cacatua galerita triton, while the bird with the salmon-colored crest is Cacatua moluccensis. Photo by S. Kates. **Facing page:** Cockatoos are easily tamed and easily trained. These Cockatoos are being put through their paces at the Paradise Park in Hawaii.

A Cacatua galerita *inside the cage is visited by an* Eolophus roseicapillus.
Photo by Raý Hanson.

A trio, from left to right: a Lesser Sulphur-crested, a Moluccan and one of the smaller sulphur-cresteds (sometimes called a Medium Sulphur-crested). Photo by Dr. E.J.Malawka.

Above: *A pet shop owner celebrates Halloween with a funny mask which is found to be very entertaining by the* Cacatua galerita. *Photo by Robert Pearcy.* **Facing page:** *A friendly* Cacatua galerita, *the Sulphur-crested Cockatoo, owned by the world-famous parrot trainer, Risa Teitler. Photo by Dr. Herbert R. Axelrod.*

BLUE-EYED OR SPECTACLED COCKATOO

(Cacatua ophthalmica)

Not available commercially, this species attains about 18 inches in length, and has a broadly set feather crest (round or circular crest) and large, intensely blue eye ring Export of the Blue-eyed Cockatoo is prohibited, almost all specimens in Europe are in the possession of zoos. Their breeding, however, has already been achieved successfully on many occasions.

Above: *The Blue-eyed or Spectacled Cockatoo, Cacatua ophthalmica. Photo courtesy of Vogelpark Walsrode, Germany.*

Facing page: *A Sulphur-crested Cockatoo, Cacatua galerita. Photo by Michael DeFreitas.*

Two views of the same lovely Blue-eyed Cockatoo, Cacatua ophthalmica. This bird has been on display in the San Diego Zoo for many years. Photo courtesy of the San Diego Zoo in San Diego, California.

Two Blue-eyed Cockatoos, Cacatua ophthalmica. *The photo above is the famous San Diego Cockatoo. We are indebted to the San Diego Zoo for this photograph. The Blue-eyed Cockatoo on the facing page was photographed by David Alderton, the author of the most complete parrot book in the world, THE ATLAS OF PARROTS.*

SALMON-CRESTED OR MOLUCCAN COCKATOO
(Cacatua moluccensis)

This species is restricted to the southern Moluccan Islands, Indonesia. It can attain 22 inches in length. Overall body plumage is delicate salmon pink. The intensity of the red coloration, however, varies greatly. Besides specimens with wonderfully pink plumage, there are also birds with only weakly reddish coloration, which can appear almost white at first glance. The reason for these differences in plumage coloration is not exactly understood. It is certain, however, that neither age nor sexual differences account for

Facing page: The Salmon-crested Cockatoo, cacatua moluccensis. *Photo by P. Leysen.*

them. The crest is broadly set in front and is normally not carried erect. It is erected only in states of excitement, such as when the birds meet each other

A Salmon-crested Cockatoo, Cacatua moluccensis. *Photo by Carol Thiem.*

or their owner or when they take on a threatening posture. The crest feathers are intensely red underneath. In contrast to other "White Cockatoos," the sexes of the Salmon-crested cannot be told apart by eye color.

Salmon-crested Cockatoos are regularly

Risa Teitler, who wrote many books about parrots and was the trainer at Parrot Jungle for a long time, trained this Salmon-crested Cockatoo to fly to her when she called it. This is a fully feathered bird. Its wings have not been clipped. Photo by Dr. Herbert R. Axelrod.

Risa Teitler has trained many Cockatoos for the famous Parrot Jungle in Miami Beach, Florida. She trains them to do many tricks, including riding a small bicycle. Photo by Dr. Herbert R. Axelrod.

available on the market. If you acquire a young bird, then you can quickly tame it. To the author's knowledge, only a few have been successfully bred.

Right: *A Salmon-crested Cockatoo,* Cacatua moluccensis. *Photo by Carol Thiem.*

Facing page: *Risa Teitler's trained Salmon-crested Cockatoo riding a bike at the Parrot Jungle in Miami Beach, Florida. Photo by Dr. Herbert R. Axelrod.*

Above: A Salmon-crested Cockatoo showing his ability to look larger than he is to scare away aggressors. Photo by S. Kates. **Facing page, left:** A lovely Salmon-crested Cockatoo. Photo by Robert Pearcy.

A mature male White Cockatoo, Cacatua alba. Photo by S. Kates.

WHITE COCKATOO
(Cacatua alba)

The White Cockatoo is somewhat the same form as the Salmon-crested Cockatoo, but smaller and with pure white plumage. It comes from the northern islands of the Moluccan group. It attains a length of up to 18 inches. Its very large round crest is pure white. The underside of the wings and the tail feathers are light yellowish.

Although this species is regularly offered for sale, it has never become as popular as the Salmon-crested Cockatoo. Even older birds that are captured in the wild become tame, and some learn to talk after a short while. Unlike some other Cockatoos, the White has been bred

You can easily see why this Cockatoo is called the White Cockatoo. Everything is white except the feet, eyes and beak. Photo by Dr. Herbert R. Axelrod.

successfully many times. Among those that were bred in captivity are a surprising number that were kept as household pets for years, and also a few that were recently captured.

This White Cockatoo gets along well with this kitten. Cockatoos get along well with most domesticated animals like dogs, cats and children! But they should never be trusted alone with any of them since they might innocently be injured or attack their 'friends.' Photo by Robert Pearcy.

This V/hite Cockatoo, Cacatua alba, *was allowed to fly freely around the house. Then it found tne crystal chandelier to its liking and began chewing the crystals loose! Photo by Robert Pearcy.*

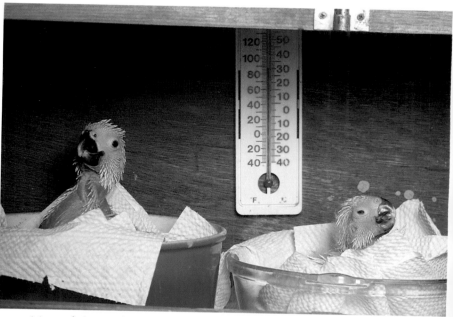

Most of the Cockatoos bred in captivity are raised away from the parents in brooders like this one. The chicks are cradled in bowls and covered with paper toweling to protect them from drafts. The inside of the brooder is kept at about 88 degrees F. Photo by Isabelle Francais.

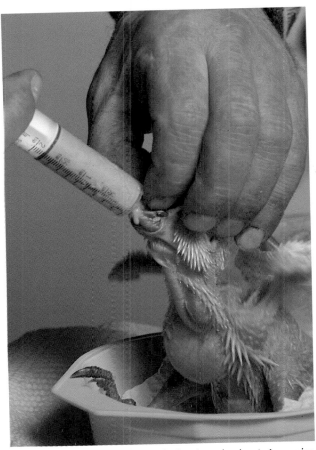

The baby White Cockatoo is being hand-raised. A precise amount of food is fed on a regular schedule. The schedule varies with the bird's size and age. There is a wonderful bond developed between the feeder and the bird, who identifies the feeder as its mother! Photo by Isabelle Francais.

This 36-day-old White Cockatoo baby has feathers which are just starting to open. Photo by R. Small.

A White Cockatoo 47 days old and weighing 350 grams, or about three-quarters of a pound. Photo by Ralph Kaehler.

A 100-day-old White Cockatoo displays to a 65-day-old White. Photo by R. Small.

Facing page: White Cockatoo, eight months old. Photo by Ralph Kaehler.

This White Cockatoo is only 82 days old and it is already displaying!
Photo by Ralph Kaehler.

RED-VENTED OR PHILIPPINE COCKATOO
(Cacatua haematuropygia)

This small Cockatoo attains a length of only 12 inches; it is a typical forest inhabitant found in the Philippines, wherever the original vegetation still grows. The plumage color

These Red-vented Cockatoos, Cacatua haematuropygia, are being sprayed. They enjoy the bathing tremendously, as do almost all Cockatoos. Bathing or spraying is excellent for the health and welfare of your bird. Photo by Dr. E. W. Burr.

of adult birds is white, perhaps with yellowish ear markings. The small crest is set forward and is usually carried laid back. The crest feathers are yellow underneath, rump feathers are red, and tail feathers are yellow underneath. The sexes can be told apart by the eye color: the iris of the male is dark brown, and that of the female is reddish brown. The Red-vented Cockatoo's red coloration develops only with the approach of sexual maturity; in young birds, these feathers are light salmon pink until the birds become a good two years old.

This formerly very rare species became more and more available in the 1970s and 80s. Young specimens are tamed quickly, and their voices, which are not overly loud, are only rarely heard. They are rather lively as aviary birds; unfortunately, keeping this species is not simple. Disorders in their moulting process, which are not yet understood, are quite frequent. A further problem associated with attempts at breeding is often the great aggressiveness of the male towards the female.

Facing page: Red-vented Cockatoos, Cacatua haematuropygia. *Photo by Dr. E.J.Malawka at the Busch Bird Sanctuary, Van Nuys, California.*

Goffin's Cockatoo, Cacatua goffini. Photo by Robert Pearcy.

A Goffin's Cockatoo. Photo courtesy of Vogelpark Walsrode, Germany.

it the smallest Cockatoo species. Plumage coloration is predominantly white. Head feathers and the small round crest are delicately reddish. Wings and tail feathers are yellowish underneath. The naked eye ring is light bluish. The male's iris is black, and the female's brownish red. Bill and feet are light horn color.

Young Goffin's Cockatoos are extremely attached to their owners. The population of these Cockatoos in their native forests on the Tanibar Islands is unfortunately being threatened by illegal deforestation. There are good possibilities, however, that aviary lines of this

GOFFIN'S COCKATOO
(Cacatua goffini)
The maximal 11-inch size of Goffin's Cockatoo makes

***Facing page:** A Goffin's Cockatoo,* Cacatua goffini. *Photo by T. Tilford.*

A Red-vented Goffin's Cockatoo in a carrying case. The food offered is very ripe fruits which have enough water to keep the Cockatoo from becoming thirsty. Photo by Michael DeFreitas.

Facing page: *The Red-vented Cockatoo,* Cacatua haematuropygia. *Photo courtesy of the San Diego Zoo.*

A close up of the face of a Goffin's Cockatoo. Photo by Robert Pearcy.

Above: Goffin's Cockatoos can extend their necks in a rather absurd fashion. Photo by Michael DeFreitas.

species can be bred in Europe, independent of imports. Reproduction of Goffin's Cockatoos in aviaries is relatively simple.

Despite their small size, they have a strong desire to gnaw, which must be taken into consideration when building aviaries.

Facing page: A drawing from many years ago of a Goffin's Cockatoo.

Below: A two-week-old Goffin's Cockatoo. Photo by Fred Harris.

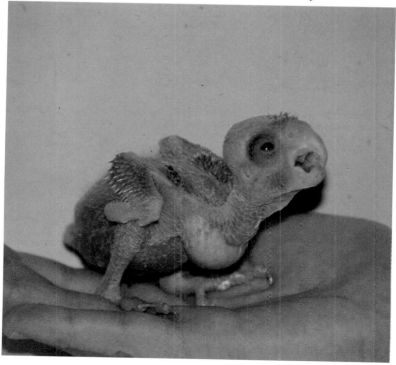

A four-week-old Goffin's Cockatoo. The pin feathers begin to cover the bird's body. Pin feathers are those feathers which haven't opened yet. Photo by Fred Harris.

A six-week-old Goffin's Cockatoo. Its pin feathers have opened and the bird begins to look like a parrot. Photo by Fred Harris.

A pair of Goffin's Cockatoos screaming in defiance as the photographer threatens their youngster, who takes up a position below the pair. Photo courtesy of Vogelpark Walsrode, Germany.

DUCORPS'S COCKATOO
(Cacatua ducorps)

Ducorps's Cockatoo attains a length of up to 12 inches. Feather coloration is pure white, with yellowish under the tail and flight feathers. The naked eye ring and feet are grayish white. Iris is black in the male, and reddish in the female. This Cockatoo from the Solomon Islands has been brought to Europe only very rarely. The author does not know whether it has yet been bred in captivity.

A Ducorps's Cockatoo, Cacatua ducorpsii, *preening itself. Photo courtesy of Vogelpark Walsrode, Germany.*

Cacatua ducorpsii. *Photo from the San Diego Zoo.*

A Little Corella or Bare-eyed Cockatoo, Cacatua sanguinea. *Photo by S. Kates.*

LITTLE CORELLA OR BARE-EYED COCKATOO
(Cacatua sanguinea)

This Cockatoo attains an average length of about 15 inches. Plumage coloration is predominantly white with delicate reddish feathers on the head and throat. It has a small round crest. The broad gray to gray-blue naked eye ring is particularly noticeable. Bill and feet are horn color. The subspecies *C. s. normantoni* from New Guinea is usually the one offered for sale. It differs from the Australian *C. s. sanguinea* by having less pronounced red on its head and throat.

Since aviary breeding is successful more often with the Australian subspecies, it is offered for sale from time to time in the bird magazines. Sexes are difficult to discern and

Above: A pair of Little Corellas with their two babies. **Below:** After being threatened in his nest box, the male comes out fighting mad. Photos by Vogelpark Walsrode, Germany.

Above: *The male Little Corella feeding his fully feathered baby.* ***Below:*** *The pair of Little Corellas keep reinforcing their bonding instincts with mutual preening. Photos courtesy of Vogelpark Walsrode, Germany.*

cannot be told by the iris color. If individuals are compared, the females can usually be recognized by their somewhat smaller size, their more slender bill base, and their narrower naked eye ring.

Despite the morose or surly appearance caused by their broad naked eye ring, Bare-eyed Cockatoos can be very lovable housemates. Young birds become tame quickly and are passionate talkers.

A wild Little Corella, Cacatua sanguinea, *photographed in its natural habitat. Photo by M. Bonnin.*

Little Corellas of the subspecies Cacatua s. sanguinea *drinking in a shallow man-made lake at Fogg Dam, near Darwin, Australia. Photo courtesy of Vogelpark Walsrode, Germany.*

The Long-billed Cockatoo or Corella is scientifically known as Cacatua tenuirostris. Photo courtesy of the Vogelpark Walsrode, Germany.

LONG-BILLED COCKATOO OR CORELLA
(Cacatua tenuirostris)

Besides the already mentioned Blue-eyed or Spectacled Cockatoo and the Ducorps's Cockatoo, this is the third species of "White Cockatoo," and like the first two it can hardly be considered for keeping by bird fanciers. Its greatly threatened natural populations are strictly protected, and there is a ban on their export. The few which are in Europe almost exclusively belong to zoos. Breeding in captivity has, as yet, been

Facing page: *The Long-billed Corella,* Cacatua tenuirostris.

unsuccessful.

Long-bills have white plumage and a red band across the front of their throat. Another red zone runs from the base of the upper bill to the naked eye ring. The unusually long upper beak is used as a digging implement. Corellas can grow to be as large as 16 inches.

Facing page: A close up of a wild Long-billed Corella, Cacatua tenuirostris, photographed in Australia by Dr. Gerald Allen. This is an endangered species now.

Above: Because this Long-billed Cockatoo is threatened with extinction, San Diego Zoo and other institutions are attempting to breed them and release the young back in the wild. Photo by the San Diego Zoo.

GALAH OR ROSE-BREASTED COCKATOO
(Eolophus roseicapillus)

Galahs belong to the genus *Eolophus*. They are, however, closely related to the species of the genus *Cacatua* and have been successfully crossed with

Facing page: The Galah or Rose-breasted Cockatoo belongs to the closely related genus Eolophus. These birds were photographed in Singapore by Dr. Herbert R. Axelrod. Singapore has the wonderful Jurong Bird Park, where many threatened species, as well as the Galah which is not threatened with extinction YET, are bred.

Galah peering out of its nesting cavity near Mildura, Victoria, Australia. The pair peeled off the lower part of the bark so predators could not climb up and get their youngsters. Photo courtesy of Vogelpark Walsrode, Germany. This subspecies is E. r. roseicapillus.

A pair of Galahs, Eolophus r. assimilis, *photographed in the wild in the center of Australia near Alice Springs. Photo by Vogelpark Walsrode, Germany.*

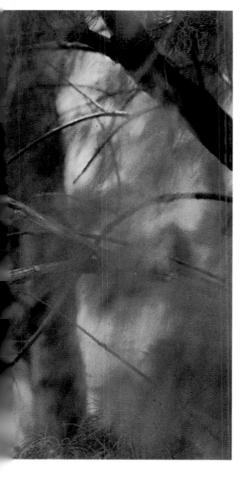

them—for example, with the Sulphur-crested, Lesser Sulphur-crested, and Major Mitchell's Cockatoos. Besides *E. r. roseicapillus,* there are two other subspecies which have been described, namely *E. r. assimilis* and *E. r. kuhli.* For the layman, however, differentiation of the three subspecies is hardly possible.

In nature, Galah Cockatoos are distributed over large parts of the Australian continent, and are quite populous in some areas. In many instances they have followed man and settled in parks and gardens. But because their export is banned, they are rarely on the market. Since breeding them in aviaries is not particularly difficult, young aviary-bred Galahs are offered from time to

species is the differently developed so-called "eye rose." This consists of a red naked eye ring of a warty nature, which is more pronounced and more intensely colored in males than in females.

Young Galah Cockatoos are quickly tamed and usually learn to speak a few words. Older birds, on the other hand, always remain somewhat shy, which is unimportant, though, because even shy birds have often been bred successfully. I know of a case in which an imported bird was bred and raised its young as early as the year following its arrival to the aviary.

The naked gray eye ring easily identifies this subspecies as the Galah *Eolophus r. assimilis. Photo courtesy of Vogelpark Walsrode, Germany.*

Galahs raised in captivity. Photo by Louise Van der Meid.

Facing page: The Galah, Eolophus
roseicapillus, *photographed in Australia.*

The Galah, Eolophus roseicapillus, *photographed in Singapore at the Jurong Bird Park by Dr. Herbert R. Axelrod.*

The Galah with its crest erected. Photo courtesy of Vogelpark Walsrode, Germany.

This Galah is half asleep. Photographed at a bird farm in Holland by P.Leysen.

NON-PET COCKATOOS

The Cockatoos previously illustrated and discussed are, more or less, available from pet shops and breeders. Other Cockatoos, due to their declining natural populations, are protected by international treaty, and trade in them is forbidden. Only zoos and other special situations receive permission to import these wild birds.

The Palm Cockatoo, Probosciger aterrimus, *a protected species. Photo by Guy van den Bossche.*

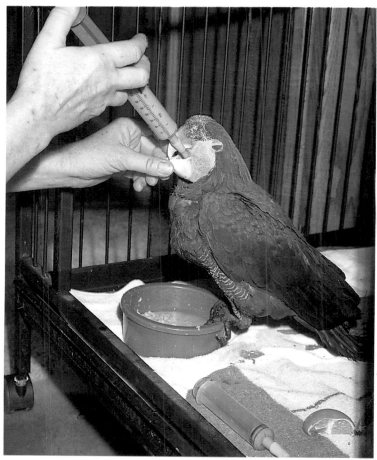

Facing page: A pair (?) of Palm Cockatoos, Probosciger aterrimus. Photo by S. Kates.

Above: A young Palm Cockatoo being hand fed. This youngster was raised from an egg. Photo by Robert Pearcy.

A *Black Cockatoo*, Calyptorhynchus funereus. *This is a species threatened with extinction. Photo courtesy of the San Diego Zoo, San Diego, California.*

A pair (?) of Black Cockatoos, Calyptorhynchus funereus. *Photo by L. Robinson.*

A flock of Red-tailed Cockatoos (C. m. magnificus) in flight. The sexes can easily be distinguished by the differently colored tail bands. These are an endangered species. Photo courtesy of Vogelpark Walsrode, Germany.

Male Gang-gang Cockatoos have the bright red crest and head feathers. Photo by Thomas Brosset.

Facing page: A male Gang-gang Cockatoo, Callocephalon fimbriatum, with a well developed filamentous feathered crest. Photo courtesy of Vogelpark Walsrode, Germany.

This is a terrible way to sell birds. Two species, Cacatua sulphurea *and* Cacatua haematuropygia *in a filthy environment. Don't buy birds from a cage as poorly kept as this one. Photo by Earl Grossman.*

Before You Buy

You should thoroughly consider all aspects of buying a pet before making your purchase, especially if it is the first time owning an animal. Nothing would be more wrong than to succumb to the beauty or charm of a Cockatoo in a pet shop and on sudden impulse to buy it. If you do not have any experience or even any information on the characteristics and habits of the kind of bird you're buying, you can be in for unpleasant surprises.

When you shop for a bird, keep in mind that Cockatoos, like all other parrots, are social birds which have a great need for socializing. If they are kept as individual birds, then you must assume the role of companion. Naturally this is only possible if you're commonly at home, or have someone there. Any Cockatoo will be miserable if left alone all day, especially when shut in a small cage. If you don't have the necessary time and still don't want to do without a Cockatoo, then either acquire a pair right off or at least provide for suitable company. Smaller

Cockatoos often get along well with other parrots such as similarly sized Amazons and African Grey Parrots. Ask your pet dealer to suggest a suitable playmate for the Cockatoo.

Many Cockatoos, particularly the larger species, have considerable vocal volume, and they scream especially when they get bored. This not only disturbs your own tranquility but may perhaps also bring complaints from neighbors. One really can't predict which bird is going

Facing page: A loving pair of Major Mitchell's Cockatoos, Cacatua leadbeateri. *When a pair is so beautiful and is so fully feathered, you can be assured they were well cared for and should be purchased if they are for sale. Photo courtesy of Parrot Jungle, Miami, Florida.*

to be a screamer: even among the largest species there are birds which almost never make use of their vocal volume.

Cockatoos make more "dust" than most other members of the parrot family. This "dust" is a fine powder created by the breakdown of the special friable powder-down feathers. The powder provides the parrot with a waterproofing agent, which in some other birds is created in a rump gland; in parrots, however, this gland is either absent or atrophied. When keeping the larger Cockatoo species,

The Galah, Eolophus roseicapillus, *in flight. Photo by Irene and Michael Morcombe.*

The Palm Cockatoo, Probosciger aterrimus. *Photo by R. Hanson.*

this powder is soon spread to all objects near the Cockatoo. Frequent sprinkling or showering can control much of the problem of keeping the powder from spreading throughout the room. The Cockatoo will also appreciate the spraying, for almost all of them like to shower. The powder problem, however, cannot be completely eliminated.

Cockatoos are great wood destroyers, transforming every wooden object sooner or later (but always systematically) into toothpicks. Of course, almost all parrots gnaw to keep their beaks worn down, but Cockatoos gnaw more than most! Therefore, the wooden perches on the Cockatoo's stand will need replacing often. These birds must not be allowed on

A Galah, Eolophus roseicapillus, atop a natural perch, from which it has been stripping the bark. As Cockatoos are natural gnawers, branches provide occupation, help keep the bill in trim and even have some nutritional value. Photo by P. Leysen.

This Lesser Sulphur-crested Cockatoo, Cacatua sulphurea citrinocristata, *is chewing on a fig leaf. Many leaves of house plants are detrimental to the health of birds, especially those leaves which have been sprayed against insect infestation or which have been fed systemic insect control chemicals. Photo by S. Kates.*

your good furniture unless they are supervised.

Never acquire a bird of the parrot family in the absolute belief that you'll have a good talker, least of all a Cockatoo. You can find talkers from time to time in all species, and most young birds may learn a few words. In general, their urge to imitate rarely approaches that of the Amazons, not even to mention African Greys.

WHY A COCKATOO?

To summarize briefly the characteristics that make Cockatoos so popular as pets, we'll first mention the esthetic impression made by these birds. The "White

Facing page: A Lesser Sulphur-crested Cockatoo screaming for attention. Many parrots get bored unless kept busy at all times. Photo by the San Diego Zoo.

Cockatoos" (of course, plumage in good condition) are a magnificent sight. Other parrot family members may be colorful and gorgeous, but Cockatoos are simply beautiful. Don't let that lead to considering such a beautiful bird as a suitable

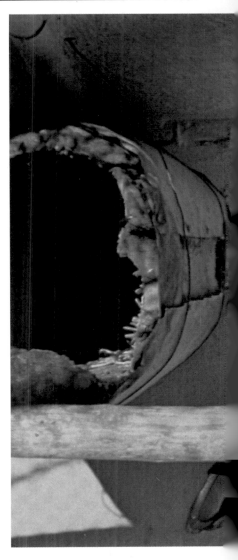

A pair of Palm Cockatoos inside a large cage at the Jurong Bird Park in Singapore. They were given a large barrel in which to nest and they succeeded in chewing several inches from the wooden edge of the barrel. Photo by Dr. Herbert R. Axelrod.

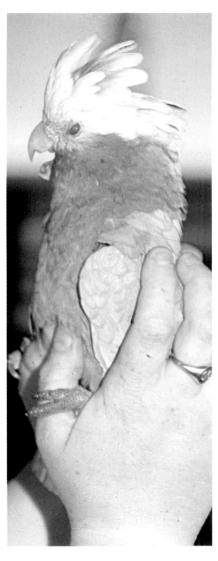

Left: *This is a rather clumsy way to hold a Galah,* Eolophus roseicapillus. *Photo by Ray Hanson.*

ornament for a still unfilled corner of a room! Don't forget for an instant that we're dealing with a living creature with social and environmental requirements.

There are hardly any other parrot family members who are as approachable as Cockatoos, which applies quite particularly to the larger species. Even if many individuals of other members of the parrot

Facing page:*This Sulphur-crested Cockatoo,* Cacatua galerita, *is preening itself. A light chain is attached to its foot to keep it from wandering off, even though its wings have been clipped. Photo by Dr. Herbert R. Axelrod.*

Playing dead is a very difficult trick to teach a parrot because it is an unnatural position for them. This bird is a Sulphur-crested Cockatoo. Photo by S. Kates.

family become tame and friendly, it's really the Cockatoos who are most likely to become really tame. Even older birds captured in the wild usually become tame after some

Facing page: *Ann Nothaft with her tame and trained Sulphur-crested Cockatoo,* Cacatua galerita. *Photo by John Daniel.*

time and patience, although it should be mentioned that this tameness is often restricted to a definite person or persons.

For people who want an animal to pet and fondle but who cannot keep a cat or dog, a Cockatoo can be ideal. The condition is, however, that those people must have a great deal of time available to spend with their Cockatoo. The free time available to the average working person is really insufficient. I know of several cases in which single

Risa Teitler, author of many books on parrots, trained birds at the Parrot Jungle in Miami, Florida. She is shown here 'introducing' a Masked Lovebird, Agapornis personata, *to a large Cockatoo. These introductions are necessary. Photo by Vince Serbin.*

Be sure you REALLY know your Cockatoo before you try anything like this. A slip and the bird will naturally bite right through your lip!

working people bought Cockatoos. After a while, the birds, who were left alone during the day, began to scream and screech so much that the neighbors complained. Whenever I'm asked for advice about that problem, I always recommend getting a second bird. In my experiences, this solution has always proved successful, which demonstrates to us how important social interaction is to a Cockatoo. Some individuals, however, don't express their feelings of

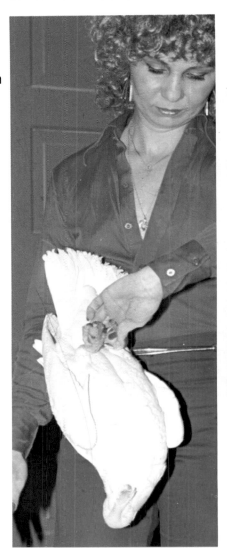

This is a natural trick since Cockatoos often hang upside down. Photo of Ann Nothaft by John Daniel.

loneliness and abandonment by screaming; they merely become melancholy, or even resort to plucking their feathers.

Despite their powerful beaks, Cockatoos rarely bite. The danger of being bitten, if you get too close, in reality is far greater with

Above: *A Salmon-crested Cockatoo,* Cacatua moluccensis, *perched on a bare arm. Scratches from the Cockatoo's sharp claws are unavoidable. Wear a long-sleeved shirt when holding a bird like this. Photo by Carol Thiem.*

Facing page: *This Sulphur-crested Cockatoo was a wild bird which became tame and begged food from people eating in this restaurant in Australia.*

African Greys and Amazons than with Cockatoos. The largest species are, by nature, the purest pacifists. However, when brooding, an otherwise completely tame Cockatoo can become aggressive, even towards its trusted owner.

Speaking of broods, of all large members of the parrot family, Cockatoos are the ones that most often breed and raise young under human care, which is certainly another reason why parrot lovers prefer Cockatoos to other members of the parrot family. The decision to buy a Cockatoo is also affected by the fact that many Cockatoo species are hardy and can spend most of the year in an outdoor aviary. In climatically favorable places, a few species can even spend the whole year

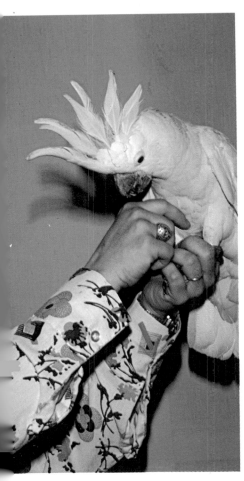

A beautiful Sulphur-crested Cockatoo, Cacatua galerita, learning to climb from one hand to another. Photo by Glen Scott Axelrod.

outside if the aviary has a shelter.

If after serious consideration you have reached the decision that the Cockatoo is the choice household pet for you and your lifestyle, then go ahead and acquire one. Remember, however, that buying a bird with the long life expectancy of a Cockatoo may well be a lifelong acquisition!

HINTS ON COCKATOO SHOPPING

Once you've decided to buy a Cockatoo, remember that every acquisition of a living creature involves problems, especially for the nonspecialist. The best start is to go to a well-managed pet shop, or to a professional or private breeder, and find out all about keeping a Cockatoo.

Be wary at first of very precise statements concerning the age of a Cockatoo offered for sale, because the real age is rarely known except in exceptional cases. It is possible, however, for an experienced eye to tell the age from the iris color of young birds of a few species up to about the second year. For other birds, however, even a specialist cannot be certain about age. It is therefore best to purchase a bird with reputable breeding records.

Above all, take enough time to shop. Observe the Cockatoo from a distance and possibly at different times of the day. Cockatoos have active and passive periods during the daily cycle. In the middle of the day they take their siesta. In the early morning hours and late afternoon they are particularly active. If you come too close to the cage, a Cockatoo stretches and ruffles its feathers.

If you have a bird fancier friend who can go with you when you buy your bird, then his experienced eye can spot defects right away which you would not recognize by yourself. You should pay particular attention to the following items:

Facing page: A Black Cockatoo, Calyptorhynchus funereus. *Photo by Dr. Herbert R. Axelrod.*

1. Plumage: The plumage should not have any bald spots. Birds just released from quarantine are often a little disheveled, which is quite normal, but the plumage should not have any newly formed feathers that are crooked or malformed. New feather pips or little bumps which are still closed should not show any dark or black coloration.

2. *Nasal Openings*: Nasal openings should be open and dry. Don't buy birds with a runny nose or with sticky or closed-up nasal openings.

3. *Bill or beak*: The margins of the upper and lower parts (jaws) of the bill should match each other well. Seen from the front, an imaginary vertical line should run down the middle of the upper and lower halves of the bill.

4. *Feet and nails*: On normal birds of the parrot family, toes 1 and 4 reach to the rear, and toes 2 and 3 reach forward. The horny leg and toe scales should be even, without any raised edges. Look to make sure all the toes and nails are present. Toe or foot injuries occur often in members of the parrot clan. For a pet bird, such damage is secondary, but it is a good reason to ask for a reduction in price. For breeding purposes,

Facing page: A Salmon-crested Cockatoo, Cacatua moluccensis, beginning to puff up and display. This defensive pose makes the bird appear much larger than it really is, thus discouraging aggressors. Photo by Glen Scott Axelrod.

however, foot defects in the males of some species could make breeding difficult or even impossible.

5. *Eyes and eyelids*: Eyes should be clear, and the eyelids, clean. Don't buy birds with wet (that is, runny) eyes, or with eyelids which are scabby or stuck together.

6. *Droppings*: The droppings of healthy members of the parrot family are solid and whitish green in color. However, frightened birds, for example, those just captured or grabbed, tend to have diarrhea.

7. *Body constitution*: Determination of the general body build is difficult for a nonspecialist because of the plumage that hides it. A bird with normal body build has a vaulted or convex chest, and a breastbone roundly padded over with chest musculature. You can check the breastbone only on very tame birds without having to hold them. Although checking the bird's weight can be useful with other members of the parrot family, it only has a limited usefulness in evaluating Cockatoos, which often show great individual differences in size even within the same species. The following body weights have been determined for Cockatoos:

Goffin's Cockatoo: 7 to 9 oz.

***Facing page:** Before buying a Cockatoo examine it closely. If the bird is tame, you should hold the Cockatoo and examine its feathers, eyes, nostrils, beak, feet and personality.*

Lesser Sulphur-crested and Red-vented Cockatoo: 9 to 12 oz.

Little Corella Cockatoo: 10 to 13 oz.

Sulphur-crested Cockatoo: 25 to 32 oz.

Salmon-crested Cockatoo: 25 to 34 oz.

White Cockatoo: 19 to 25 oz.

It is recommended that you weigh your Cockatoo in its cage, as in this way you can weigh your bird without terrifying it. First, however, you must know the weight of the cage and its basic contents when empty of the bird. Then simply weigh the cage with bird in, and subtract the weight of the empty cage.

LEGALITIES AND REGULATIONS

All imported members of the parrot family must go through a quarantine period upon arrival in most countries; they are kept isolated and receive preventive medication during that time. The purpose of quarantine is to prevent the introduction and spread of diseases which would be dangerous to man and other animals. Legally imported and quarantined parrots are fitted with a closed leg band bearing a serial number. This band is proof of legal importation and

Facing page: If you can afford it, buy two birds of the same age and same species, preferably young birds which were hand raised. This will give you the chance to breed them (if they turn out to be a pair...a 50% chance), and the birds will keep each other company when alone. Photo by Ralph Kaehler.

should not be removed unless absolutely necessary. If its removal becomes necessary or (as can occur with the larger Cockatoos) the bird itself succeeds in biting it off, then save it or its remaining pieces. When you buy from a pet shop or from a reputable breeder, the band number as well as the name and address of the buyer should be recorded in a registry.

A Lesser Sulphur-crested Cockatoo, Cacatua sulphurea, *in a cage with suitable wire. Wire like this affords maximum viewing and enables the Cockatoo to climb, giving it much-needed exercise. Photo by Carol Thiem.*

There is often very strong bonding between humans and Cockatoos. The bird is a Galah. Photo by Ray Hanson.

Accommodations for Your New Cockatoo

On the subject of accommodations, it's a truism that a parrot cage is often too small but can never be too big, which is particularly so for lively birds such as most Cockatoos. Parrot cages with a floor measuring of 18 x 18 inches and a height of

This sturdy bird cage is especially designed and manufactured by one of the world's leading pet supply manufacturers. Only buy a parrot cage from a pet shop as the wire, solder, spacing and servicing are extremely important. Many parrots have died of lead poisoning because the solder used was poisonous and was soft enough to be eaten. Photo courtesy of Hagen Pet Supplies.

24 to 28 inches cannot be used even for the smallest species, unless the birds can leave the cage regularly throughout the day. To lock up in a small cage such a lively and mentally well-endowed bird as the Cockatoo is plain and unvarnished cruelty to animals. On the other hand, a cage with a 32 x 24-inch floor and a height of 35 to 40 inches suffices either for a pair of the smaller species of Cockatoo or one large Cockatoo. Even with that size of cage, however, it is good to let tame birds out for awhile each day.

A parrot stand with removable cage cover manufactured by Bird Depot, Inc.

If you have a choice between vertical and horizontal bars on the cage, the horizontal ones are better because the Cockatoo can climb them more easily. The lower part of the cage, including the drawer-like pan, is best made of metal. Lower parts of the cage made of hard plastic or similar material can be used only for the smallest species. In purchasing a cage for a Cockatoo, look for a very solid design. Many

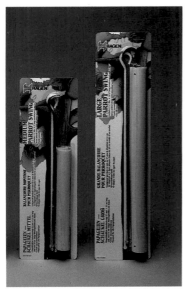

about two-thirds of it. Only in that way can the nails be worn down naturally on the wood, thus avoiding excessive nail growth and the need for nail clipping. Perches are quickly gnawed away by most birds and must be replaced regularly. For some individuals it is best to use hardwood

A swing inside your cockatoo's cage will provide it with many hours of enjoyment. The proper swing can be found at your local pet store. Photo courtesy of Hagen Products.

A modernistic parrot stand with removable cage cover. Photo by Bird Depot, Inc.

individual birds, especially the larger species, are accomplished masters at cage demolition.

Each perch in the cage must be so thick that the bird's foot can only encircle

perches, such as beech or oak. In no case should you replace wood with any other material (such as metal) for perches to be used by inveterate gnawers.

Designed after the Parrot Jungle outdoor perches. Parrots cannot climb above the hood. Photo by Bird Depot, Inc.

This is a magnificent cage for a Cockatoo. Below is a secure, heavily wired cage, while on top is a play pen. Photo by Bird Depot, Inc.

Gnawing is necessary for the normal wearing down of the bill in all members of the parrot family. If they are kept from gnawing or don't

Various types of hanging perches, to match any decor, are available at pet shops. Photo by Bird Depot, Inc.

find anything to gnaw, then excess bill growth or malformation is often the result. Smaller Cockatoos such as the Galah Cockatoo or the Lesser Sulphur-crested Cockatoo may not exhibit a great need to gnaw. For the larger species, such as the Salmon-crested, White and Sulphur-crested Cockatoos, however, it may be necessary to use particularly hardwood for perches. An excellent material which far

exceeds the durability of hardwood, is air-dried stem portions of juniper bushes. They are not only hard, but are also rough, so that our "hookbill" has something to bite.

A convenient cage is provided with feeding cups which can be serviced from the outside of the cage. There should be four food cups, rather than two of them, and they should be either stoneware or stainless steel.

The drawings show different sizes and styles of perches. Cages should have different sizes and styles so the toes do not become cramped from staying in the same position all the time. Think of the various sized branches in trees and you will get the idea.

CLIMBING ACCESSORIES

A climbing apparatus made of several transversely or diagonally arranged perches can be set up on the cage roof. Again, all of these perches should be too thick for our bird's toes to go all the way around. If the perches are too thin, the nails will begin to show excess growth from sticking out in the open air and not being worn down on the perch.

If there is enough room, you can erect a climbing post next to the cage (instead of the apparatus on top of the cage). Good woods include knotty or gnarled branches from hard, leafy trees such as oak, beech, and maple, and even pine tops. The base of the climbing post can be a large Christmas tree stand or the base of a garden umbrella.

AVIARIES

Think about whether you can remodel the corner of the room where the cage is going, and instead of merely placing the cage there, build an inside aviary. It not only gives your housemate more freedom of movement but is also the ideal place to try to breed your birds. The easiest way to start is to have two solid walls available. Even with only a few square yards of floor space, and a room height of about seven or eight feet, you can put together an aviary which is preferable to most any cage. Since Cockatoos, however, will hardly leave whitewashed or plastered walls alone, you have to cover the walls. You can use tin, or if only smaller

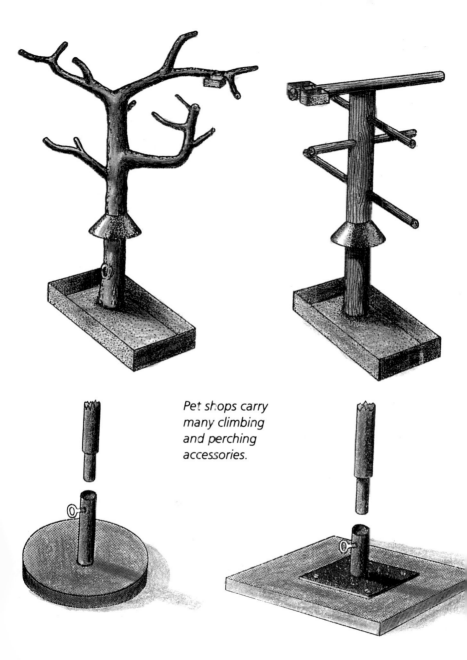

Pet shops carry many climbing and perching accessories.

species are involved,
formica or a similar material
used on kitchen counters;
the edges have to be
finished with gnaw-proof
metal strips. The open sides
of the aviary are closed with

*Heavy-duty water and feed
dishes are necessary for
Cockatoos as they will try to
chew them up, as they chew
everything within range. A
suitable attachment is also
necessary so they cannot tip out
the contents of the dishes.*

metal-rimmed welded mesh
screens. A doorway goes
into the lower portion.
Small doors in several places
can be useful for feeding or
for suspending nesting
boxes. For smaller species
use spot-welded metal
mesh with a wire thickness
of 1.2 to 1.5 mm. For larger
species use a wire thickness
of 2.5 to 3 mm. For
constructing smaller
aviaries, pet shops supply
ready-made mesh sides with
and without doorways.
These sides may not always
be in stock but can be
ordered, even to your

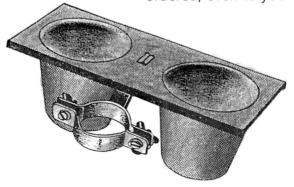

While it is possible to buy outdoor aviaries, you might find it more enjoyable to build your own. The design below is suitable for all birds, but the wooden edges must be protected, as the Cockatoos will surely chew on any exposed wooden edges.

specific measurements.

Finally, it has to be pointed out that electrical lines, lighting, etc., have to be carefully protected by armored cable and wire baskets.

The arrangement of perches, climbing devices, etc., is up to the imagination of the owner. The feed and water containers have to be placed so as to avoid soiling. The floor of an indoor aviary, too, should be covered with tin, turned up at right angles about 4 to 6 in and very close to the mesh. The floor is best covered with sand. In setting up the aviary, avoid everything that gets in the way of easy cleaning.

Pay particular attention to all door catches because Cockatoos are often routinely active in breaking out, and patiently open most locking devices once they learn how to do it—usually just a small padlock helps. Similarly, aviaries can also be built in the yard or garden. The construction of such outdoor aviaries requires thorough preparation, especially if they are to be used permanently. Entry of predators and rats must be prevented by a concrete slab foundation. One or, better, two closed walls are desirable. A detailed description of the construction of outdoor aviaries, shelters, etc., would lead us too far afield here, so refer to the professional and technical literature.

For summer, small outdoor aviaries can be set up with modest means on a balcony or a terrace. Being outdoors is very healthy for all Cockatoos and has a very favorable effect on their plumage.

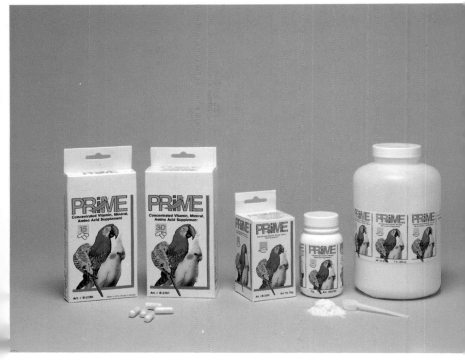

To ensure that your pet cockatoo is receiving the proper vitamins and minerals, it is a good idea to add some type of supplement to its diet. Ask the clerk at your local pet store for assistance in choosing which one is right for your type of bird. Photo courtesy of Hagen products.

Above: An outdoor aviary designed to hold several pairs of Cockatoos. The photograph on the facing page is similar to the design shown above. **Below:** Lesser Sulphur-crested Cockatoo, Cacatua sulphurea. Photo by Carol Thiem.

From this aerial view of an aviary, you can see the roofed and unroofed parts of the flights, which communicate with a solidly enclosed shelter. Photo by David Alderton.

Unfortunately, even the best kept birds can fall ill. Medication for the most common ailments is good to have on hand. Many different broad-spectrum antibiotics are available from your local pet store. Photo courtesy of Hagen Products.

Proper Feeding

  With their crop, well-developed glandular stomach, powerful gizzard, and other digestive organs, Cockatoos are first and foremost granivores (seed eaters). The Cockatoo beak is splendidly suitable as a husking and cracking organ. Ripe as well as germinated seeds are almost always hulled. Usually only green seeds are eaten with the coat. Besides grain, seeds of all kinds, nuts, and similar items, wild Cockatoos also eat many fruits, green plant parts, and often insects and their larvae. Cockatoos cannot live on sunflower seeds alone.

As far as their diet goes, Cockatoos are creatures of habit. The feeding of Cockatoos captured young often involves a problem caused by unbalanced diet. It can be very difficult to get a Cockatoo used to a balanced and wholesome diet when, as a young bird, it grew up on an unbalanced diet.

Older–captured Cockatoos tend to be less one-sided in their feeding habits. They are typically curious and are more likely to try various foods offered to them, as I've seen in numerous observations of birds under quarantine. Birds fed only one kind of food when young can very stubbornly refuse all foods they don't know. These Cockatoos require a lot of patience and sensitivity to accustom them to a broader diet. You should always try to get your Cockatoo used to a varied diet.

SEEDS: Seeds suitable for Cockatoos can be divided roughly into two groups,

Facing page: One of the easiest ways to befriend a Cockatoo is to hand feed it. Photo by Robert Pearcy.

namely carbohydrate-rich seeds and oil seeds. The carbohydrate-rich seeds include cereals such as barley, oats, and wheat, as well as rice, corn, and numerous kinds of millet and buckwheat. The oil seeds include—besides the very commonly used sunflower seed—hemp seed, nuts, pumpkin seed, and peanuts (which belong to the legumes). Smaller oil seeds such as rape and niger are not taken by Cockatoos. Almonds, on the other hand, are welcome delicacies for most Cockatoos.

Fully ripened rice and corn are eaten only rarely. Many Cockatoos like puffed rice very much, and boiled rice is an important diet item for sick birds. Some Cockatoos don't like unhusked oats but will eat them husked. Most Cockatoos like millet, despite the small size of the grains.

GERMINATED SEEDS: Many of the seeds mentioned above can be eaten not only ripe but also green and germinated. Most birds, for example, relish half-ripe ears of corn. Wheat and sunflower seeds are particularly suited to germination. Germinating seed as food for members of the parrot family must be governed by the same strict hygiene guidelines as for human food. Mold on germinated seed can lead to a serious illness. Besides the seeds mentioned above, many Cockatoos also like to eat germinated peas. Germinated seeds are recommended especially during breeding.

BASIC DIET: The basic

mixture of ripe seeds should contain, at the most, 50% sunflower seeds. The remaining 50% can consist of whatever your own Cockatoo likes, such as oats, millet, and other carbohydrate-rich seeds. If other oil seeds are mixed in, then the amount of sunflower seed has to be proportionately reduced.

Although hemp seed is liked by almost all Cockatoos, don't mix in too much of it. Hemp seed contains, depending upon where it was grown, more or less harmful substances

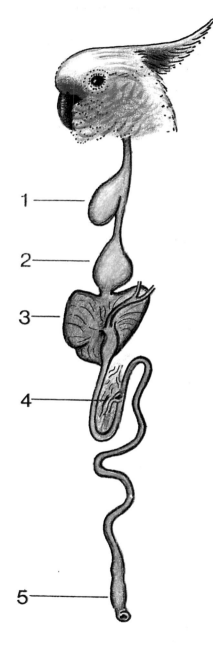

THE DIGESTIVE ORGANS OF A COCKATOO

1. The crop.
2. The proventriculus.
3. The ventriculus.
4. The duodenum.
5. The cloaca.

of which too much can be dangerous. Neither should large amounts of nuts, which are high in fat content, be fed to the Cockatoo; the nuts are really relished, but should be given only now and then as treats. Green hazelnuts, if you can find them, are usually preferred over ripe nuts.

The shelf life of carbohydrate-rich seeds is best under dry storage conditions. Their vitamin content drops rapidly, however. Nuts and similar oily seeds, on the other hand, cannot be stored too long, or they become rancid. Rancid oil-rich seeds are unsuitable as feed and, if they are eaten, can be very dangerous for the birds. Every bird owner should make it a habit to carefully check the

Suitable food for a Cockatoo includes most fruits and vegetables cut into small pieces—and they must be absolutely fresh. Photo by Fred Harris.

sunflower and/or other oily seeds when shopping for bird feed. You can often see and smell any rancid seeds immediately. Many fanciers recommend germinating a sample of the seeds before feeding—seeds that do not sprout are considered unfit for consumption.

With the help of these recommendations and your own testing, it should not be difficult to devise the appropriate seed mix for your own bird.

GREENFOOD (FRESH VEGETABLES): Most Cockatoos love fresh greens. And, as we mentioned, they also like green seeds, so there's a potential for continuous alternating of diet between green seed and green foods. You can add even a little more variety to the

diet by freezing half-ripe ears of corn and keeping them for winter treats. (Remember to thaw them out before giving them to your Cockatoo. If you have a garden, you can also sow some millet and then feed the green seeds to your bird or freeze them for use later during the winter. Other green foods, besides the old standby chickweed, are lettuce, endive, dandelion, and spinach. As for berries and other fruit, you can

Facing page: Spray millet is enjoyed by all birds, even the larger species such as a cockatoo. These nutritious treats can be found at your local pet store in various quantities. Photo courtesy of Hagen Products.

give anything the bird likes. Then there's also bananas, carrots and other root vegetables; potatoes should be cooked before feeding them to your Cockatoo. Unripe, that is, still green, wheat and oats are also a welcome change in diet.

A good supplemental food to satisfy your bird's urge to keep busy consists of fresh branches from fruit trees, willows, poplars and linden trees. The buds will be bitten off, the bark peeled off and nibbled, and one or the other will be eaten in the process. Never use any vegetables or tree branches sprayed with insecticides!

VITAMINS AND TRACE ELEMENTS: These substances are vital. Birds that receive a good seed mix plus daily greens and fruit as supplements are hardly in danger of suffering vitamin or trace element deficiencies. Birds, however, who have a one-sided diet of seeds and who largely refuse other foods, may do better if they receive a properly dosed multivitamin preparation in their drinking water. Once they get used to eating greenfood and fruit, you can easily discontinue the vitamins.

MINERAL FEED:
Minerals are an important part of complete nutrition. Mineral mixes used for pigeons or ornamental birds are suitably formulated for Cockatoo health. You can also use grit or grit blocks, which are sold in pet shops. Mineral substances such as sand and grit or fine gravel grains should always be accessible to the bird, for these are swallowed with

A mixture of fresh seeds like sunflower, corn and even peanuts, are ideal supplementary foods and can be offered in heavy-duty seed cups. Photo by Dr. Herbert R. Axelrod.

the feed from time to time and facilitate digestion in the gizzard, which functions somewhat like a millstone.

ANIMAL FOOD: Wild Cockatoos eat various amounts of animal substances. These foods, such as insect larvae, contain large quantities of high-quality proteins. Unfortunately, the insects (mealworms, for example) normally bred as feed for other animal pets are not suitable for Cockatoos, who hardly touch them anyway. Two readily available protein foods which Cockatoos will usually eat are hardboiled egg and dog pellets or biscuits. Also available are high-protein pellets for members of the parrot family. Ask at your pet store about them. These items are normally given as supplements once

or twice a week. In general, don't increase the protein content of feed unless the birds are breeding.

TABLE FOOD: Table food is very important to all tame bird pets. The question often asked by bird lovers, "What can I give my Cockatoo from the table?" can be answered as follows: Assuming that not much table food will be given to the Cockatoo, especially not any salty or spicy foods, you can give the Cockatoo some of just about anything. In this author's experience, Cockatoos gnaw—often with great passion—pork chop bones, nibble on mashed potatoes and on fried fish, and will even try whipped cream. This kind of gormandizing is not dangerous and often very

Tearing off the branch of a fruit tree not only affords your Cockatoo the chance for some fresh fruit, but they will have fun tearing the branches and leaves apart, making quite a mess, too.

wholesome. Only, as already mentioned, don't exaggerate, especially with dairy products such as cheese, which many birds like to eat. Give only small pieces now and then. Too much cheese can cause digestive upsets caused by the cheese casein balling up in the crop.

Lesser Sulphur-crested Cockatoo, Cacatua sulphurea, *eating a peanut. Photo by A.J. Mobbs.*

Two Major Mitchell's Cockatoos fighting over a peanut shell. Be sure there is enough food for all the birds so they don't become competitors for food. Photo by Dr. Irvin Hoff.

Cockatoos make strong bonds with people or with other Cockatoos. An expression of 'love' is the mutual preening ceremony where the birds preen each other, as shown here. Photo by David Alderton.

The New Home

A newly acquired bird should be left in peace awhile when first brought home. It can leave its cage once it is familiar with its surroundings. Only if you've acquired an already tamed Cockatoo can you let it out of the cage on the first day. Imported birds, too, may already be tamed when you get them, in which case they may have been taken from the nest and raised by humans. In the countries which export them, the breeding and raising of birds are woman's work; thus many such birds are "women's birds," meaning they are especially fond of women.

Even if your imported Cockatoo does happen to prefer women, though, it usually won't be unfriendly to men. Note, however, that such affinity toward women is often misunderstood, as it has nothing to do with the Cockatoo's own sex.

Move slowly and carefully around the cage of all birds that are not yet tame. In a few days you can try to approach your new pet. Your voice helps to make friends with your Cockatoo. Speak softly as you feed it and as you carry on your regular activities near the cage. Cockatoos, like all other members of the parrot family, quickly learn to distinguish the voices of different people.

Once the Cockatoo's best human friend (whoever he turns out to be) appears and the bird calms down and sits still, you can begin handing it tidbits such as

Facing page: Risa Teitler, famed author of parrot training books, with two Cockatoos, Cacatua galerita *and a* Cacatua moluccensis. *Photo by Dr. Herbert R. Axelrod.*

almonds, peanuts, etc. Don't neglect offering it food every day, even if several days or weeks pass before your bird takes the first piece of food from your hand. Almost every Cockatoo's natural need for social contact will cause it, sooner or later, to overcome its instinctive caution.

After the Cockatoo learns to take food from your hand and is comfortable, you can try carefully to touch it. Getting your bird to let you touch it is easier if approached through the social feather grooming pattern in the Cockatoo's behavior. These birds are markedly social in grooming and preening their feathers, which they often do mutually. In the absence of another bird, your Cockatoo may let you scratch it. For the best chances of success, try at first to touch its forehead near the base of the beak. It learns fast that your gently scratching hand is not dangerous, and it may soon stretch out so you can scratch the back of its head, too. In these attempts at approaching the bird, do not make the mistake of wearing gloves (as it may bite if you do). Cockatoos, like all other imported larger parrots, panic when they see gloves. The reason is that during the quarantine period, when they were banded, examined, etc., they were seized by hands wearing heavy gloves. A Cockatoo thus associates the gloves with unpleasantness.

In the beginning, do everything to enhance the bird's confidence in its owners (especially its

Two friendly Cacatua galerita, *Sulphur-crested Cockatoos. Photo by Fritz Prenzel.*

favored person).
"Tameness" is directly related to the bird's confidence in its human friends. It takes sensitivity and time to build confidence, but any built-up confidence can easily be destroyed by doing something wrong, especially in the beginning. It is absolutely wrong to lose your patience with a bird that is still unfamiliar with your household. Patience, and patience alone, achieves the desired tameness.

Properly integrated into the household, almost all Cockatoos not only become tame but may become so pushy that now and then they can really get on your nerves. In such cases, at least with the larger species, a friendly tap or flick on the beak sets it straight, which a really tame Cockatoo catches on to very fast.

As a rule, a family Cockatoo will not treat all family members the same, as it tends to show a preference for one particular member.

HOW TO HAND CARRY A COCKATOO

A Cockatoo with clipped wings that is fairly familiar with its surroundings can be let out of its cage. If it tries to fly and crash-lands on the floor, you don't have to attempt to recapture it with your hands. Just set the upper part of the cage over him.

It's usually easiest to have the Cockatoo climb onto your hand from the floor, which takes advantage of the bird's discomfort at being on the floor of a still unfamiliar place. In its effort to get up a little higher and so have a better overview of things, it may take your outstretched hand as a first step onto the broomstick lying right there at its feet. Once on the pole, the way to your hand is not far.

This lady likes parrots! On her shoulder is a Blue-fronted Amazon, Amazona aestiva. *The Cockatoo is a Salmon-crested,* Cacatua moluccensis, *while the bird with its back to us is a Blue-and-yellow Macaw,* Ara ararauna. *Photo by Carol Thiem.*

step upwards. This step can be made psychologically easier for a still shy bird by holding an inanimate object such as a short pole, rod or broomstick for the bird to climb on. It simply has to

SMALL CHILDREN, DOGS, CATS

Questions one often hears about Cockatoos are: How does a Cockatoo act towards small children? Are there difficulties in its getting used to other household pets such as dogs and cats, or vice versa?

Small children should not be put in contact with a still shy Cockatoo at first. The threatening posture, especially of the large Cockatoos, is usually so terrifying that even precocious children will scarcely try to grab or hold the bird, but a certain amount of caution is good at the start.

Dogs usually get along well with the larger parrots, and this applies just as well to Cockatoos. Once they get used to each other, dog and Cockatoo can even become friends. Every dog owner, of course, must know what to expect of his dog. No real problems can be expected in getting a well-trained dog used to its new housemate. It's usually easier to introduce a Cockatoo that already lives in the household to a newly arrived puppy. A Cockatoo can almost always count on being respected when it takes on its harmless threat posture towards a still uncertain new arrival, like a puppy.

On the other hand, the Cockatoo–cat combination is somewhat a problem. All cats, programmed by nature to be solitary predators, possess a marked hunting instinct and so should not be left alone unsupervised even with a large member of the parrot family. Many Cockatoos, but not all, react with sheer terror even in the mere presence of a cat in the same room.

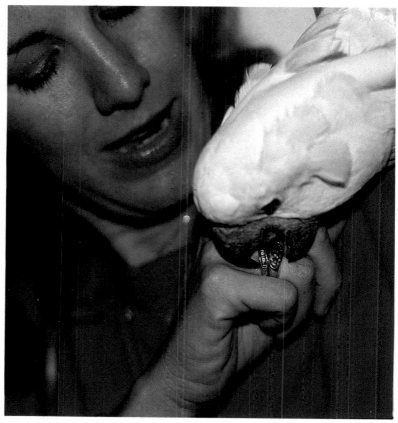

Cockatoos are often attracted to shining things like gold rings. It can be pretty painful to the owner of a ring if a Cockatoo decides to tear it off!

A leg chain can be used to confine a Cockatoo to a certain area. However, the danger of leg injury is great, and some Cockatoos object strenuously to this method of restraint. Many fanciers believe that an enclosure is the only humane means of confinement. Photo by S. Kates.

Cockatoo Care

Cockatoos don't demand too much of their owners besides daily feeding and fresh drinking water, the receptacles of which have to be washed out every day. Remember that in the warmer time of the year it takes only a few hours for drinking water to turn into a bacterial culture.

Bird cages are cleaned at least weekly. About every month, cages and perches are scalded with hot water. Cage sanitation is made easier when droppings are removed from the cage or aviary floor on a daily basis and those spots strewn with clean sand. Coarse sand (1 to 2 mm diameter grains) is sufficient to cover the floor of the cage or aviary. Gnawed perches have to be replaced from time to time; Cockatoos will even gnaw through the perch or branch on which they are sitting!

COCKATOOS LIKE SHOWERS

All Cockatoos like regular showers. Regular showering helps to keep their plumage clean and glossy. Showers also help cut down the messy spreading around of the fine powder which is constantly made from the powder-down feathers. Shy birds should be sprayed carefully with an atomizer or other water sprayer, such as used to moisten indoor plants. Once used to it, birds happily follow you into the bathroom to be showered off with a hand-held shower device. In the summer, outdoor birds can be carefully showered with the garden hose. Shower water should always be about 77° to 86°F.

NAIL TRIMMING

If toenails grow excessively long, despite thick perches, trim them accordingly. Cut them with a nail clipper as you would do for a dog's nails. If the nail begins to bleed, you have cut too close, cutting

The proper place and angle at which to cut a Cockatoo's nails (claws). Don't cut too short or it will bleed. If possible, hold the nail up to the light so you can see the blood vessel in the nail and avoid cutting it.

into the blood vessel. Apply an antiseptic and styptic powder. To prevent excess nail growth, use perches too thick for the bird to close its toes around completely; the Cockatoo should just be able to grasp it two-thirds of the way around, thus regularly wearing down its nails. You can also give your bird perches of various grip strengths to exercise its leg muscles.

WING CLIPPING

Aside from birds meant for breeding from the very start, clipping the wings of a new arrival can make taming easier because a bird whose wings are clipped cannot simply fly away when you approach. Clipped wing feathers regrow after awhile, so the Cockatoo eventually regains its normal ability to fly.

Imported birds almost always have their wings

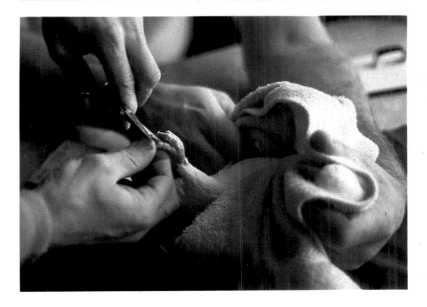

clipped. If not, you can ask the pet shop dealer how to go about having the flight feathers clipped. If the pinion feathers are merely shortened, the disadvantage is that you can see the clipped feather ends when the bird sits. It's better to clip the feathers in such a way that the uncut outside feathers, as seen in

Above: *The Cockatoo should be firmly held in a heavy towel, with its head immobilized, while you have someone clip its nails. Photo by Dr. E.W.Burr.*

Facing page: *Using the same towel-holding technique, the feathers in the wing can be cut in the same manner as the nails but with a different scissors. Photo by Michael DeFreitas.*

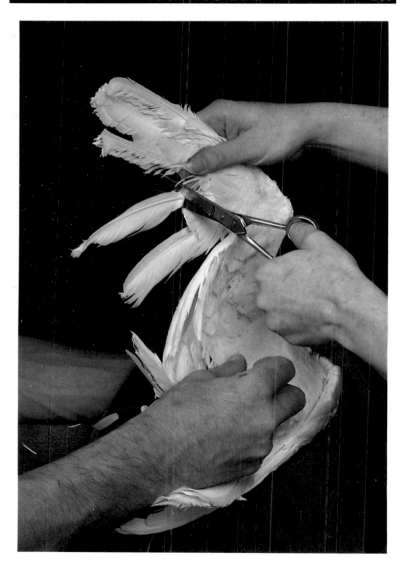

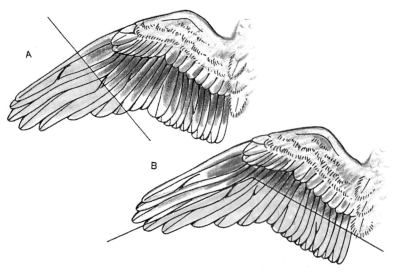

Alternate feather trims: Removing the primary feathers (above) very effectively curbs flight, but the wings are unsightly when folded. Leaving the outer primaries intact (below) and clipping the secondaries produces a more pleasing appearance but may still permit flight, depending on the ability of the Cockatoo.

a sitting bird, cover the cut ones.

In general, it can be mentioned that Cockatoos are by nature better flyers than, for example, African Grey Parrots or even Amazons. If you improperly clip a healthy Cockatoo still in full possession of its vigor, the bird just might manage to take off and reach a nearby tree. Even if you can almost always retrieve the runaway bird, its escapade usually generates a lot of undesirable excitement and anger. You can trust clipping when it's done properly and as long as regrowing feathers are kept clipped. It's a good idea to keep an eye on the pinion feathers so they can be clipped on time. On a really tame bird, it's not difficult to clip back the proper

Untamed or agitated Cockatoos can best be restrained for examination by using two hands and a towel, with one hand controlling the head and beak. Photo by Dr. E. W. Burr.

feathers gradually with short, strong scissors.

A LITTLE RECREATION

A little bit of occupational therapy is part of a Cockatoo's daily care. This is particularly important when the bird does not have another bird to keep it company. A good way to provide occupational therapy is to give the Cockatoo fresh twigs or branches daily. These kinds of branches have already been mentioned earlier in the section on feeding.

Many birds can also keep busy with balls of yarn, wooden balls and so on. Usually, however, wooden toys are all chewed up after some time and have to be replaced. Some Cockatoos also like to climb vertically, on a hawser, thick rope, or chain hanging down from the climbing apparatus on top of the cage. Aside from twigs and branches, which can be nibbled and chewed up, and which almost every Cockatoo enjoys, the selection of toys is very personal—simply make a few little tests and find out what your Cockatoo likes to play with.

TEMPERATURE AND HUMIDITY

The routine of ongoing care includes checking on temperature and humidity. Cockatoos in general are insensitive to low temperatures. They usually even tolerate great differences in temperature without any apparent discomfort, but with the proviso that the temperature differences do not occur suddenly. Acclimated birds kept in outside aviaries can stay there until the first night's frost occurs. The winter temperature of 41° to 50°F in the shelter (which is built into the aviary) is adequate.

Newly imported birds from countries with tropical rain forests (that is, birds like the Lesser Sulphur-crested, Salmon-crested, White, Triton, Red-vented, and Goffin's Cockatoos) would do best with longer periods of acclimatization. The important thing is to avoid drafts. Drafts and the body cooling associated with them are, in practice, much more dangerous than all other mistakes. Even the selection of the site for the cage in a room or the construction of an indoor aviary requires some attention as to how to ventilate the room without exposing the bird to drafts.

With combination outside-and-inside aviaries, the entrance/exit opening should be about midway up (or down). That's because the birds like to sit way up on the inside wall— assuming you've installed a suitable place to perch there—and they will be out of any direct draft through the opening.

Many Cockatoos come from markedly arid regions, and even the species from tropical rainforests are not particularly sensitive to dry air. In European and American temperate climates, birds kept outdoors will always have sufficient air humidity. If, however, room air humidity drops below 50% in the house, which is quite possible with central heating in the winter, the Cockatoo's feathers can become brittle after a while. Since too low an air humidity is unhealthy for people too, you can provide an air humidifier in the interest of your pet, as well as yourself.

Above right: The Red-tailed Cockatoo Calyptorhynchus magnificus magnificus. Photo courtesy of Vogelpark Walsrode, Germany. **Below:** Galah, Eolophus roseicapillus. Photo by David Alderton.

Behavior

Cockatoos are skillful climbers and, besides having climber's feet, use their beak as a trace-hook or pintle, serving as a third foot. They frequently use a foot as a hand, as for example, when holding fruit with a foot while it's being eaten. On the floor they move along rapidly and purposefully despite their waddling gait. In nature, wild Cockatoos, especially Australian species, feed to a large extent on the ground. A few species, for example, the Sulphur-crested Cockatoo, hop along on both feet, which for members of the parrot family is almost an unknown mode of movement.

A peculiarity due to the Cockatoo's natural environment, which must be taken into account when keeping them, is their terrified reaction to suddenly appearing shadows or light, and unexpected noise. When these things happen, Cockatoos often in panic try to fly—flying into obstacles they know are there, such as screens, windows, etc.

This behavior is particularly marked in species that come from steppes or prairies. In those places, natural cover is lacking, so flight is the only recourse to escape enemies. If in your home headlights can suddenly flash through your windows, then light-proof curtains or shades will help. Cockatoos with unclipped wings are extremely skillful and maneuverable fliers. If you let them fly free around the house, they avoid every obstacle, and even when

Facing page: The wonderful historical painting of the Glossy Cockatoo, Calyptorhynchus lathami, *by J. Gould, reminds us of the abundance of this creature at one time...it is now faced with extinction.*

landing hardly hit anything.

Adult and healthy Cockatoos sleep on one leg. Couples and other birds used to one another sleep close together. While they are sleeping, they are somewhat ruffled. The head is often turned back and the front part placed in the dorsal plumage. Aviary birds almost always go back to the same spot to sleep. The young birds, for a while after they first leave the nest, sleep perched on two legs. In moving parallel to the perch, the bird sidesteps or moves one foot ahead of the other, setting it down in the long direction of the perch). The tail feathers are lifted somewhat or angled away to the side in a downward direction.

A healthy Cockatoo spends quite a bit of time in preening itself. The bird scratches around busily, using its foot to groom the head feathers that lie out of the reach of its beak. In general, Cockatoos scratch upwards with the foot. Galah Cockatoos can be observed now and then scratching themselves like Cockatiels do, that is, bringing the foot backwards over the wings, coming up from behind to scratch the head. The rest of the plumage is groomed thoroughly every day. In doing a good grooming job, Cockatoos can assume the oddest positions to reach all of their feathers. Birds which get along well together, especially those living as mates, help each other in grooming. This social preening also plays a ritualistic role in breeding pairs.

Cockatoos, just like all

Sulphur-crested Cockatoo, Cacatua g. triton, *preening itself.*
Photo courtesy of Vogelpark Walsrode, Germany.

other members of the parrot family, feed each other—an activity which occurs regularly with couples. This mutual feeding, or attempts at it, can also be observed from time to time among birds who are merely social, not breeding, partners. Tame birds, especially those imprinted on man (raised by human beings), may show their affection for their human friend by attempting to feed him. The bird brings up the partially digested food from its crop, and feeds its mate or partner with that regurgitated food. In the process the donor bird takes the recipient bird's beak in its own beak to make the transfer of food.

DO COCKATOOS LEARN TO TALK?

If you place particular value on a talking member of the parrot family, then I would not recommend your buying a Cockatoo. You might find a passionate talker among the Cockatoos now and then, but in general the Cockatoo's urge to mimic speech is not as developed as, for example, in the Amazon and African Grey Parrots. Really good talking Cockatoos are the exception rather than the rule. If your newly acquired Cockatoo begins to imitate human words, consider it a lucky buy, but don't expect a talker as a matter of course. I personally know of one very good talking Little Corella Cockatoo and also two White Cockatoos that gossip merrily together, even though they sit right next to each other—which is noteworthy insofar as talking Cockatoos often stop talking when in the company of their fellow Cockatoos.

The best chances for a talking Cockatoo are with a young bird. The owner can reinforce learning by repeating the words clearly and often. Impressive, easily remembered words of two or three syllables are imitated best. In many cases, however, even with a Cockatoo that possesses a talent for imitation, no amount of the most careful demonstration of how to pronounce words will help if your bird finds it more fun to imitate the barking of your neighbor's Dachshund. Birds with a good talent for imitation of sound may specialize in any of the possible sounds around them, from the ringing of the telephone, to the noise of the vacuum cleaner, from the striking of the wall clock, to the dripping water faucet but not in the human voice. There are exceptions, of course, as for example Cockatoos who have acquired a certain vocabulary and even appear to be able to use it in the appropriate context.

One should naturally not conclude that a Cockatoo knows what it says, even if it often uses words in the right context with other words, sounds or even activities. A good example of such behavior is when a Cockatoo says "Hello," whenever the telephone rings, "Good day" whenever anyone comes in, or "Good-bye" as soon as you put your coat or hat on. The Cockatoo often heard those words used in the context of those events. It also happens that some sounds may even be imitated in advance, for example, when the bird makes the sound of a sewing machine or a vacuum cleaner as these items are brought into the room, or when it makes the sound of water being poured when it sees you pick up the watering can. A few years ago there was a White Cockatoo television star, who lived with his master, a detective, in a series of mystery films. When the detective's telephone rang, the Cockatoo lifted the receiver and said "Hello," that is, reacted in word and action to the stimulus (a telephone ring).

Misunderstandings can occur when the bird confuses similar things. An almost classic example of a mix-up like this is what happened in the Cologne Zoo after World War II with a Sulphur-crested Cockatoo who had obvious difficulties in differentiating between various uniforms. His habit of greeting British officers with "Heil Hitler, Comrade!" was not exactly taken as an example of Cologne humor. The zoo resolved the sticky problem by arranging its "marriage." After that, the aforementioned Cockatoo spoke only with its mate, in Cockatoo tongue only.

The pertinent question of whether some species of Cockatoos have more talking members than do other species cannot be answered with any certainty. As for my own experience, I've heard Long-billed Cockatoos and Major Mitchell's Cockatoos talking, and known Galah Cockatoos who whistle and babble. But they are exceptions. When you buy a Cockatoo, it would be unwise to expect your new bird to develop into a good talker.

THE FEATHER CREST

The feather crest which characterizes the Cockatoo differentiates it from all other members of the parrot family. Only the closely related Cockatiel has a similar crest. The structure of this feather crest is not the same in all species; we can distinguish two types, the pointed crest and the rounded crest.

The back part of the pointed crest consists of a row of long feathers arched forward or upward; these feathers are erectable, but clearly stand up near the nape even when the rest of the crest is not erected. To the front, the crest is delineated by shorter covering feathers which reach down almost to the root of the upper half of the beak and rest on the head when not erect. The longer feathers of the pointed crest are of a different color than the body plumage, but the shorter ones are the same color as the body. Pointed crests adorn Major Mitchell's, the Sulphur-crested, and the Lesser Sulphur-crested Cockatoos.

Round crests consist of long and short feathers which can be flattened completely, and which are arranged by row next to each other. The underside of the crest is colored differently than the rest of the body in many species, such as the Salmon-crested Cockatoo. Round crests differ greatly in size, depending upon the species.

Salmon-crested and White Cockatoos have large round crests. Galahs, Long-billed, Red-vented and Little Corella Cockatoos have small round crests, which are usually quite broad in front.

This is a young Palm Cockatoo in perfect condition. Photo by Robert Pearcy.

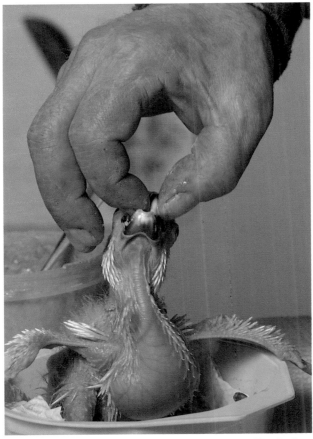

Hand raising Cockatoos is not technically difficult, but takes a lot of time. Either you do it professionally, raising lots of Cockatoos or other parrots, or you are retired and have lots of time. Photo by Isabelle Francais.

Breeding

Many Cockatoo species are so decimated in their native habitats that we've got to expect a reduction in the importation of captured wild ones. For some species, export is generally banned. Domestic breeding is helping to build up the availability of many species, such as was done successfully with various of the smaller parrots. Because the capturing process can never be an ideal way for the bird lover to obtain his birds, we should recommend breeding in every instance where there is space—aviaries are not always absolutely necessary.

The reason why Cockatoo breeding was so much more successful, even in the first years, than the breeding of other large members of the parrot family (Amazons, African Greys, and Macaws) is perhaps because there was no problem with differentiating the sexes of Cockatoos. With the exception of the Salmon-crested Cockatoo, sexing is possible for all the White Cockatoos because of the iris color or other distinguishing characteristics. These differences were described in the species descriptions earlier in this book. With the Salmon-crested Cockatoo, the veterinarian can do the sexing either with eye refraction or with laparoscopy.

Cockatoos develop slowly and become sexually mature only in the third to fifth year. If young partners get accustomed to one another, the chances are particularly good of their becoming a breeding pair. With older partners of the opposite sex who have been forced to live together, you need some luck to get them to breed productively. Be very careful when matching two birds who don't know each other, because males can be overly aggressive towards the females.

Indoors, Cockatoos can breed any time of the year, and they don't seem to be bound to any definite breeding season. Breeding fervor can be encouraged by feeding germinated seed and feeds rich in animal protein. An adequate mineral supply is particularly important. Germinated seed contains large amounts of vitamin E, which favorably affects the maturation of the sexual products. Animal protein, as a concentrated nutrient, improves general body constitution. Supplemental minerals have to be included in the diet for the formation of eggshell, and later for the skeleton of the young birds. Suitable protein, besides hardboiled egg, may include dog pellets or parrot pellets. You have to try various

foods to see what your own Cockatoo will accept.

NESTING BOXES

Cockatoos breed in nest hollows inside partially rotten tree trunks. If you can find a trunk section from a poplar, linden, or willow tree that would offer an ideal nesting site, you can leave the interior design of the rotting trunk section to your Cockatoo couple. If you can't find a trunk section, or if it can't be brought in because of space limitations, then you need a nesting box. A nesting box for Cockatoos must be made of hard material that won't quickly be chewed up. Use well-seasoned, unplaned boards at least one-inch thick. Even thicker boards can be used for breeding couples of larger species, perhaps with a

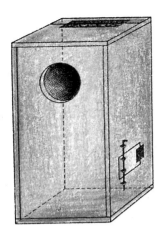

Nest boxes suitable for breeding Cockatoos are sometimes available from pet shops. Otherwise, build you own, following this sketch.

10 ¹/₂ x 15 ¹/₂ inches. For larger species, inner dimensions should be 14 x 14 x 22–24 inches. The opening to be cut into the upper third of the front should be about four inches for smaller species, and about six inches for larger species. Nesting boxes cut from reamed-out tree trunk sections are only good for the smallest species. Their inside diameter should be at least 10 inches and their height about 12 inches. A hinged roof that can be opened and a side observation port are both desirable. A strong branch nailed on a slant to the wall makes a ramp for the Cockatoo to climb into the box opening.

hardwood such as oak or birch for the front wall. Experience has shown that the birds begin to gnaw almost always on the entry/exit opening in the front wall. The size of the nesting box for smaller species should have an inner dimension of 10 ¹/₂ x

No species of white Cockatoo uses nesting material. Birds in the wild lay their eggs on the wood remnants which form the floor of a natural tree hole. The moisture-retaining material from the inside of moldering trees is the best lining for the nesting box. Many people take a mixture of short wood shavings or coarse sawdust and peat, which, however, dries out rapidly. Partially moldered wood brought home from a walk in the woods is preferable in any case. Galah Cockatoos also use other nesting material, such as thin twigs and similar material, which they carry into the nest.

If you want to be a naturalist, find a large enough rotten tree and cut off a piece suitable in size for your Cockatoo, then hollow it out. Usually splitting the log in two, scooping out the inside and then screwing it or wiring it back together, makes the task so much easier.

COURTSHIP AND BROODING BEHAVIOR

The courtship displays which precede mating are not very pronounced in Cockatoos. You'll note that particularly newly matched couples often screech loudly, are restless, and may do some hefty gnawing, usually on the nesting box. It is conceivable that this gnawing is an instinctive replacement for the usually necessary widening of a tree hole when the bird is living wild in nature. You can often observe very busy mutual grooming, but also threat posturing and bowing with erect crest.

The behavior of birds which have been paired for some time is often only hinted at or is even absent altogether, especially if they have bred together before.

When the mating itself is occurring, the female at first assumes a patterned typical position. She sits somewhat ducked down and completely still, with

A hatchling Sulphur-crested Cockatoo which has been artificially incubated. Photo by Frank Nothaft.

A 4-day-old chick covered with down. Photo by Vogelpark Walsrode, Germany.

after the first egg is laid, the young will hatch at corresponding intervals. This explains the characteristic differences in the size of the young of all members of the parrot family, which can be seen during the first weeks of development following the laying of several eggs.

Smaller species generally

The same chick at 18 days shows it has lost its down and opened its eyes. Photo by Vogelpark Walsrode, Germany.

her lowered wing tips trembling. Because the actual mating is relatively long and can last several minutes, it can hardly be missed. During the height of the breeding season, this process is repeated often.

The eggs are usually laid over a period of several days, but since the birds generally begin brooding

In 25 days the feather shafts are coming out of the skin. Courtesy Vogelpark Walsrode, germany.

lay an egg every second day, while larger species lay one every fourth day. Smaller species usually lay three or four eggs, while larger species usually lay two eggs. This is, however, only a general rule, and many exceptions can occur. Galah Cockatoos, as well as Major Mitchell's Cockatoos, have often been known to lay up to six eggs.

Brooding time is 22 to 24

This 32-day-old chick can't even fit in the dish any more. It screeches with fright at having been removed from the nest box. Photo courtesy of Vogelpark Walsrode, Germany.

At 40 days of age, the feathers are opening and the crest is already becoming evident. Photo by Vogelpark Walsrode, Germany.

days for the smaller species, and 26 to 30 days for the larger ones. Both Cockatoo parents usually share the brooding, the male during the day and the female during the night. Frequent relief during the shifts, however, also occurs. There are at least some pairs in which the female broods alone for the first days, and she is fed during this time by the male.

THE NURSERY

The hatchlings are fed from the crop, at first by the female and then somewhat later by both parents. No special feed is necessary for the young, assuming, of course, that the diet is varied, which

At 42 days, a Cockatoo chick is already a personality! Photo by Don Mathews.

should be taken for granted during every breeding session. Besides the usual feed, hygienically acceptable germinated seed, fruit, and green vegetables are recommended. Many breeding pairs also like peas (soak them if dried) and fresh corn (or defrosted frozen corn).

The development of young Cockatoos lasts, depending upon the species, 50 to 90 days, until they leave the nest box. Aside from the species differences, the developmental time can depend to a certain extent upon the number of young. A single young bird naturally grows somewhat faster than it would if it had to share food with nestmates. In large broods, the smallest young birds may starve. In nature, it seems that such "extra" young birds from third or fourth eggs are merely insurance for unfertilized eggs or for eggs damaged during brooding. In breeding captive birds, however, the breeder can save these birds by rearing them artificially. Long after they leave the nest, the young will still be crop-fed from the parents for quite some time. The young can usually take most softer food or germinated seed by themselves. When broods follow one another, such as can occur with Galah Cockatoos, the male feeds the young for a while by himself.

SOME ADVICE

To what should the breeder pay special attention during the breeding season? The first rule is to avoid disruptions. If the female is somewhat nervous, then let the cage housecleaning go for the duration of the brooding. It's also important to maintain a humidity of at least 60%, especially inside the nest box. Most

Cockatoos, however, help maintain the necessary humidity in the brooding hole. In the days just before the chicks hatch, the females bathe, usually quite thoroughly, carrying the wetness into the nesting box. This behavior is restricted to this short

At 56 days, this Cockatoo chick is almost fully covered with feathers. Photo by Don Mathews.

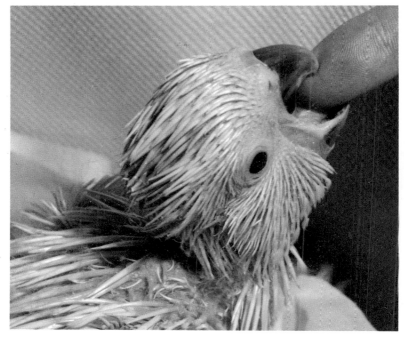

Lesser Sulphur-crested Cockatoo, C. s. citrinocristata, *38 days old. Photo by Don Mathews.*

period. At other times it suffices for the birds to be rained on or showered. So give your Cockatoo couple an opportunity to bathe.

It should be mentioned too that brooding birds can also become aggressive towards their trusted owner. So, during this period, don't count completely on the usual peaceful nature of the larger species.

Health and Safety

The beginner in bird care should leave the treatment of sick birds to the veterinarian. No matter what kind of bird you have, always find out where the closest veterinarian can be reached in an emergency. You can't take a sick bird to just any veterinarian: not every veterinarian is familiar with the treatment of ailing parrots, and real bird specialists are not that common. It's usually possible, however, to ask the nearest vet where you can find one of his colleagues who specializes in birds.

In the event that veterinary help becomes necessary, it helps to know your bird's weight beforehand. The bird's weight will determine the dosage of any medication it might receive.

Once Cockatoos are tamed and at home, they are not overly prone to illness. Severe illnesses are very rare in birds that are accustomed to our climate and care. The early recognition of any beginning illness, however, is extremely critical for successful treatment. Be attentive to changes in your bird's behavior. Changes could be the first signs of sickness. (That doesn't include, of course, changes due to mating and breeding activity.)

First Steps: The first thing to do when illness is suspected is to keep the patient warm. Warmth is a well-founded home remedy, which helps for cold symptoms, such as sniffling. A heat lamp placed over the cage raises the temperature to 88–104°F, but the bird *must* have a way to get out of the direct beam of the lamp. A dose of vitamin B added to the feed or water is also recommended for all sick birds. As soon as an illness is suspected, contact your veterinarian immediately.

COLD SYMPTOMS

Especially if a cold is accompanied by inflamed eyelids, consult a veterinarian. Inflammations are often caused by bacterial infections triggered by drafts, and may also be partially due to vitamin A deficiency. In the case of newly imported birds, the symptoms of colds and inflammations can also be associated with ornithosis (psittacosis). In either case, antibiotic treatment is called for as fast as possible. Eye infections are also treated locally with antibiotic eye ointment, that is, in addition to the overall treatment.

DIARRHEA

Diarrhea in newly acquired birds is usually caused by stress. An abrupt change in diet can cause diarrhea, in which case the diarrhea can be cleared up by several days on a rice diet. During this treatment period, the bird is given only boiled rice and drinking water. If diarrhea continues, consult the veterinarian.

SALMONELLOSIS

Infections like salmonellosis occur more easily among birds held in outside aviaries, where wild birds (also mice and rats) can transmit the disease. These infections hardly occur in birds kept inside the home. In suspected cases of salmonella infections, definite diagnosis is only possible by examination of the droppings. Treatment is prescribed by the veterinarian.

WORM INFESTATION

Worm infestation is common in birds kept outside and in newly imported birds. Worms can be transmitted by other birds. If you suspect worms, a sample of the droppings should be sent to a veterinary laboratory for parasitological examination. Any vet can give you an address. If the results of the worm examination are positive, the vet will prescribe treatment, which, depending upon the specific worms involved, often requires several treatments within a certain prescribed interval.

MOULTING

Moulting is not an illness but a completely normal process by which the old feathers are replaced by new ones. Although most birds moult during definite hormonally influenced periods once or twice a year, all members of the parrot family moult more or less over the whole year. At times, however, moulting is more pronounced in many Cockatoos, especially in brooding birds.

Moulting disorders, which are manifested by insufficient development of new feathers or by the appearance of "crippled" feathers can be due to a deficiency in dietary animal protein. If such disorders appear, then resort to supplemental feeding with animal protein, vitamins (a lot of fruit and green food) and minerals and consult your veterinarian.

SKIN AND FEATHER PARASITES

Skin and feather parasites can also cause feather

damage. These ectoparasites (external parasites) are not particularly common, but biting lice (Mallophages) sometimes occur on Cockatoos. To treat for ectoparasites, only proven safe preparations should be used. If in doubt, ask the veterinarian which insect powder to use.

VITAMIN DEFICIENCY DISEASES

Vitamin deficiency diseases hardly occur in birds which receive—and actually consume—a varied diet. For all birds which restrict themselves to only certain kinds of food, however, a standard supplemental multivitamin preparation in their drinking water is advisable.

Pay special attention to birds which show signs of acute vitamin B deficiency. This can happen to all predominantly granivorous birds if long-stored carbohydrate-rich seeds are fed to them. Since the quality of such seeds—quite apart from mineral deficiency—is hardly affected, they look just like fresh seeds when you buy them. If seeds like these are eaten by birds which also get a varied diet, then the lack of vitamins in the seeds is not important. Acute vitamin B deficiency in a bird receiving a one-sided diet, however, can quickly kill the bird.

Vitamin B deficiency is manifested by poor coordination of movement, and, in severe cases, by loss in equilibrium. In these cases, large quantities of vitamin B should be given either directly into the crop, or as an intramuscular injection. If the disequilibrium is caused by something other than vitamin B deficiency, then the dose of vitamin B will not cause any harm.

FEATHER PLUCKING

Feather plucking is, despite many opinions to the contrary, not due to deficiency; it is a psychological condition. It is not particularly frequent among Cockatoos, but it can occur here and there. Affected birds either pull their feathers out or bite them off. After a while bald spots begin to appear in the belly and chest plumage. It can be extremely difficult to make a feather plucker stop this habit. A thorough change in its lifestyle usually brings results. Association with other birds like itself is a great help.

ORNITHOSIS AND ASPERGILLOSIS

The available space in this book does not allow any detailed descriptions of all bird diseases, so those interested should consult the literature on the subject. However, two diseases which every parrot owner should know about are mentioned briefly here.

ORNITHOSIS: Ornithosis, erroneously once called psittacosis (parrot fever), is caused by the microbe *Chlamydia psittaci*. This disease doesn't run any typical course; symptoms can be varied. Sniffling, sneezing, and eye inflammations have already been mentioned, and a mucoid greenish diarrhea is not uncommon. Affected birds are apathetic, sleep a lot and puff out their feathers. Their breathing is often audible. Transmission is partially by dry and pulverized droppings in dust form, or by droplets sprayed out by sneezing. Definite diagnosis can only be made serologically from blood samples. Because this examination is time consuming, treatment with antibiotics is started upon mere suspicion of the disease. It is important to know that even healthy-looking birds can carry this disease, and that it does not only affect members of the parrot family. The preventive treatment given during the quarantine period is not a 100% guarantee that birds quarantined according to regulations will be free of ornithosis. Today, most

birds treated early survive. For birds which aren't eating or don't eat enough, the antibiotic can be injected, instead of being administered through the food.

A basic understanding of this disease is important for two reasons:

1. Ornithosis can be transmitted to human beings. Every bird owner with respiratory ailments should alert the doctor to the possibility of an ornithosis infection. In man, this infection is usually manifested by respiratory infection with grippe-like symptoms, or else as a pulmonary infection, often with high fever. The choice of the right antibiotic is important, for many of them, such as penicillin, are useless.

2. The fact that this

disease also attacks other birds suggests that transmission of the infection could involve wild birds, like sparrows, for example, which can enter an aviary through wide-mesh screening, or whose droppings can fall into the aviary. Several cases of infection from wild birds have been reported.

ASPERGILLOSIS:

Aspergillosis is another extremely malignant disease, but it occurs only rarely among Cockatoos. A widespread and ubiquitous fungus, *Aspergillus,* is the cause. It hardly affects healthy birds, infecting mostly birds which are otherwise weakened. The spores penetrate the respiratory organs (trachea, lungs and alveoli) and begin to multiply there.

Aspergillosis is always suspected when antibiotic therapy does not successfully clear up a respiratory infection. Previously we were helpless against this disease, but today we can handle it.

POISONING

Poisoning by spoiled food such as rancid nuts, sunflower seed, etc., can easily be prevented by careful shopping. Many molds and fungi can form toxic substances, so watch for moldy foods. Cereals which have not been dried sufficiently before storage can become moldy. The need for good sanitation to prevent mold when preparing germinated seeds has already been mentioned. Bitter almonds, which contain hydrocyanic acid, are extremely poisonous. Bitter almonds are more bitter than sweet or edible almonds and are only about half their size.

MEDICATION

Medications are best "laced into" the bird's favorite food, or else dissolved in the drinking water. If medications are given in the water, then don't feed any greens or fruit, which would satisfy the bird's thirst. If medication has to be administered, do it with the bird held in its natural position. The veterinarian can introduce medication directly into the crop via a tube.

All drugs and vermifuges should be given only in the dosage and method prescribed by the veterinarian. Once an antibiotic is started, it must be continued for the *whole* prescribed time and must not be discontinued before that time is over.

DANGERS IN THE HOME

A Cockatoo turned loose in the home requires watching—the same supervision needed for a small child running about. Corrosives, solvents, detergents, insecticides and herbicides, etc., should not be left standing around in the open. Quite aside from the fact that Cockatoos plus houseplants are hardly a good combination, houseplants may include poisonous species. Particularly poisonous are porcelain flower or wax plant (*Hoya carnosa*), oleander (*Nerium oleander*), Nux vomica (*Strychnus nux-vomica*), and all species of *Diffenbachia*. In the garden, as well as the yard, watch for poisonous plants: golden chain or rain tree (*Laburnum anagyroides*), *Clematis* spp., acacia-like *Robinia* spp. and yew (*Taxus* spp.).

The danger of electric cords was already mentioned in the section on aviary construction. You've got to think of the electrical connections inside the home, too, if a Cockatoo is about. Even if the danger is only slight that a Cockatoo will get a shock from a damaged cord (its horny beak and dry tongue will only conduct a small amount of current), damaged electrical wires could set fire to your home.

Finally, note that Cockatoos, just as all other birds, are extremely sensitive to fumes from solvents, paint thinners, etc. Your pet Cockatoo should

be kept away from the house when housepainting or when other such work is going on.

A male Sulphur-crested Cockatoo. Photo by S. Kates.

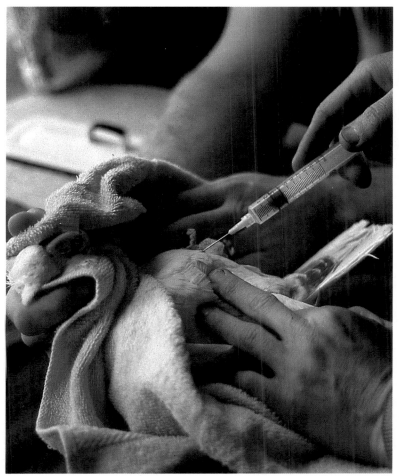

There are veterinarians specializing in birds, especially large and expensive birds like Cockatoos. This shows the technique in of parenteral injection into the pectoral musculature. Photo by Dr. E.W.Burr.

Major Mitchell's Cockatoo, C. leadbeateri. Photo courtesy Vogelpark Walsrode.

BIBLIOGRAPHY

THE WORLD OF COCKATOOS
by Karl Diefenbach.
ISBN 0-86622-034-8
More than 100 photos, 208 pages
    hardcover.
Excellent book for beginners.

TAMING AND TRAINING
    COCKATOOS
by Risa teitler
ISBN 0-86622-779-2
About 90 color pictures in 100 pages.
    The best training book ever
    written by Parrot Jungle's head
    trainer.

HANDBOOK OF COCKATOOS
by Dr. A.E.Decoteau
ISBN 0-86622-798-9
160 pages, hardcover, fully illustrated
    in color.
A very valuable guide for the
    beginner. One of the best sellers
    in the field.

PARROTS AND RELATED BIRDS
by Bates and Busenbark
ISBN 0-876622-967-4
This old favorite has sold hundreds of
    thousands over the years. It is
    constantly being updated and
contains valuable information on
    all parrots (including Cockatoos).
    Written by two of the most
    experienced bird breeders. For the
    more advanced parrot lover.

PARROTS OF THE WORLD
by Joseph M. Forshaw
ISBN 0-876622-959-3
Magnificently illustrated with lovely
    drawings by William T. Cooper,
    this has been a wonderfully
    accurate guide to most parrots as
    they exist in nature. No hybrids
    are described and nothing about
    care or breeding or training, but a
    great book for identifying parrots
    and parrot-like birds.

ATLAS OF PARROTS
by David Alderton
ISBN 0-86622-120-4
This is the best there is on parrots in
    general. Lots of information on
    Cockatoos, and everything written
    in this wonderful book is
    applicable to cockatoos.
No book could be more highly
    recommended. If you can afford
    only one book on Cockatoos, get
    this one.

INDEX

The Proper Care of
COCKATOOS

Photo by Michael DeFreitas.